BECOMING
BRAVE

A sassy woman's guide to turning fear into bravery

BECOMING BRAVE

A sassy woman's guide to
turning fear into bravery

Katie Dean

Torchflame Books
An imprint of Light Messages
Durham, NC

Becoming Brave
Katie Dean
www.yourwildlife.com.au
katie@yourwildlife.com.au

Published 2018, by Torchflame Books
an Imprint of Light Messages
www.lightmessages.com
Durham, NC 27713 USA
SAN: 920-9298

Paperback ISBN: 978-1-61153-276-0
E-book ISBN: 978-1-61153-275-3
Library of Congress Control Number: 2018930935

She wasn't looking for a knight, she was looking for a sword.

- Atticus

You don't
need anyone
to come and
save you.
You were made
for this,
and this will be
part of
what makes
you.

WHERE TO FIND THE GOOD STUFF

PREFACE

This book had to be written. She wouldn't leave me alone and was one of the most persistent passion projects I have ever encountered. These words endured. They grappled to be here. They rumbled and I softened.

Even after I lost the book completely to a not so epic move on my part, she kept on knocking, so I know this message is meant for you.

Thank you, for being the person I wrote this for.

YOUR INVITATION

So here we are. I'm heavily pregnant, my Cavoodle is at my feet and my tiny hurricane is in the bedroom next door asleep.

I've done it.

I just wrote the final chapter for this piece of sass and magic. If I do say so myself, I think it's the sh*t.

While I have written these eighteen chapters of personal poop storms and learnings, and it's technically finished, I don't think *Becoming Brave* and I will ever be *truly* done.

WHY?

Because we never really stop doing the work.

I thought I was *Brave* and knew what that was all about when I began writing these pages, but now I feel an entirely different type of bravery flooding my veins. This book has been there to guide me through the scariest thing I've ever had to do, so far.

Perhaps that was her purpose all along.

Here I was, setting out to write a book to help women just like me turn "Fear into Bravery," when in actual fact, perhaps I was writing to remind myself that I have everything I need to turn the constant fear that

I had endured into the Bravest thing I have ever done ... so far (I have to keep adding the "so far" because life has a divinely surprising way of keeping us on our toes which allows us to unlock different levels of our awesome), but more on that later.

I can't imagine what's about to go down when I bring this second babe home from hospital, but something tells me I'm not meant to know because it would scare me senseless. "Ignorance is bliss," they say, and that seems pretty OK with me for the minute. I totally have a healthy respect for THE FEAR. I have for many years. I see this undervalued emotion as the catalyst for greatness, but before we dive right in to all the shenanigans, true tales and tidbits, I want to see if you, my friend, are really up for it.

I spent a large chunk of my wild-haired youth avoiding any self-inquiry which in hindsight 'twas not my smartest move.

I avoided any feelings that I didn't understand. I numbed myself out; ran from, avoided and hid from any sign that I would have to get real with myself, and I became quite the expert let me tell you!

I thought I was living this wild and free life back then, when in fact, I was trapped. I was trapped in a cage of my own making. It wasn't until I stopped running that the adventure truly began.

The adventure to get to know myself.

The great adventure within.

GASSSSP—I know. Sounds fun, right?

In order to truly love ourselves we must first start to get to know ourselves. We must weather the shit storms this proverbial introduction is going to create. Amongst the meditations and the panic attacks, lost loves, heart breaks, breakthroughs and break downs I realized something, the journey to become your truest most authentic self really is the *wildest* ride.

All this, while I was out there chasing freedom, when the freedom I was actually craving would come in the form of permission to be myself.

I am on the journey of a lifetime and it's not something you need to do alone.

The question is, Brave Heart, are you going to join me?

Are you game?

Are you up for the wildest ride of your days?

Are you keen to join me to bring an understanding to one of the biggest doorstops of the emotional world?

For me, through the pages of this book, it really has come full circle and just like Rafiki presents Simba to the heard in the Lion King, consider this my equally extravagant handing over of what is about to come.

Cue Music.

It's the ciiiiiiiircle of Liiiiiiiiiiife.

In these pages, you are going to walk through eighteen chapters of never before shared True Tales and options to NEXT LEVEL your own life. You'll get to see a side of me that not many people do. A side that I believe we all have. As women, we are all connected and now you and I get to share *this* experience too.

You are now officially part of my movement to embrace the *F-Bomb*.

F-YEAH!

In order to live
a brave and
courageous
life,
first, you have to
allow yourself
to feel
a little
scared.

1

We All Have the Same Stuff

Fear doesn't discriminate.

I am here to help you make this all too familiar *F-Word* into a trusted forever friend. Your ally. Your compadre.

Your sign letting you know that you are on the right track. By the time, you have turned the final page of this dalliance with my four-lettered friend, you won't make any major life decisions without it. Just as the words on one of my favorite shirts quotes, "We are all connected," and this was one of the motivators for writing this book, to unite us and to create a worldwide echo of the words "Me Too."

We all have the same stuff. The details are just a little different.

There is a current theme and some sisterly solidarity amongst our stories and it is time we let it bring us together, and revel in the fact, that we are not alone.

- **We have all retreated at some point by a fear of judgment or of being judged.**

- We all worry that we aren't *enough*.
- We all want to be loved.
- We all have felt regret.

At some point, we have been fearful of failure, or on the flip side had a fear of being seen coupled with the judgment that follows suit—and, while both of those are a little different—the result is still the same.

We are kept still.

We become *stuck*.

We are kept stagnant and this is where the damage is done. If you were to take a clear flowing river of ideas and dam it up, that creative water is going to become rotten. The stench of wasted opportunities would burn your nostrils like a cup full of straight Dettol. What a waste.

We don't want to stank up our house, or burn our nostrils for that matter (thanks, Mom), so let's learn to make Fear our friend, fall in love with the mystery and use this energy source for making magic.

Let me share with you, a few different ways Fear has made her presence known to me over the years, to see if you can see yourself in any of it. When you do, and I believe you will, you will understand what I mean when I say, "We all have the same stuff."

When I look back at the way my life has gone, I spent many years being afraid. I didn't realize it at the time, but there was always an underlying element of angst and worry created by my own melon and it was always, without a doubt, in my mind—*Fear*.

Fear showed itself in many ways being the saucy emotional chameleon that she is, but the underlying flavor, was indeed, fear itself.

- I was afraid of what could go wrong.
- I was afraid of what could go right.
- I was afraid to get too comfortable.
- I was afraid to stay still.
- I was afraid to take a chance and yet the thought of not pushing the envelope petrified me even more.
- I was afraid to be with my thoughts in the quiet.
- I was afraid to be in a room of people for fear of their judgment.

I remember driving to an event I was to appear at in Sydney, many years ago, and without knowing what was going on I slowly began to implode. I didn't know it was fear at the time. I was calling it anything and everything I could think of. The mind chatter was at a roar, my stomach was in knots and it was as if I was actually in real danger.

I never made it to that event.

I never made it to a lot of events because I was petrified of everything that could possibly unfold, yet I couldn't even tell you at the time that I was even afraid. I had no idea.

I was imprisoned within a world of my own making and there wasn't an iron bar in sight. I didn't know at the time that *this* was anxiety. I didn't know that my signals had been mixed up and I was reading them wrong. I just knew that I couldn't deal and that something was epically wrong. It was as if I was forever at base camp of Everest, in a leotard ready for the climb, yet clearly, I wasn't equipped.

Life from the age of sixteen through to twenty-seven, was shrouded in doubt, limiting beliefs and heartbreak. There was always an element of uncertainty and of walking on shaky ground. There was always a fear that something bad might happen if I did, *the* thing, whatever *that* thing was.

- I would obsess over conversations long gone.
- I would look for confidence in the bottom of a Bacardi bottle.
- I would be the girl laughing the loudest but feeling the lowest.
- I would have nightmares and little sleep.
- I would comfort myself with food in the early hours of the morning, until I found myself unable to keep my eyes open falling asleep to the glow of the TV.

I knew that wasn't normal, but I also had no desire to *be* normal. I just knew that things had to be different.

Things changed.

Was there one situation that sent me on this quest for my best? Noooo, there were many. Eventually, I got sick and tired of my own bullshit story and the waves I was creating, and decided that enough was enough.

What I do know for sure is that my life flows in seasons and while the proverbial lights came on all those years ago at age twenty-seven, of late there has been another huge shift in a totally different form. It's clear that I'm still *Becoming Brave* and I become braver with each level of awareness. Each level of consciousness demands and creates a different version of us and that is something magical and evolutionary.

If you want to live a brave and courageous life then first you've got to allow yourself to be a little scared.

Some of the most pivotal points in our lives can come from us having a gut full of our own actions and these are the ones that I think really stick.

We become fed up with our own restrictive boxes we've put ourselves in.

Tired of the cages we've built for ourselves with our mindset. Tired of the never fun, but endless *judgy* finger pointing—until one day, you are standing in front of a mirror—and, the fingers pointed at you. You've called your own bluff and you have to own your place in your story.

SHIT.

Rock bottom.

Or, is it?

This is where I learned that Bravery can look like you're not actually doing anything at all, and that can also be completely terrifying.

At the end of 2015, I mentally crashed and burned. I was whistling about as loud as any kettle on a hot stove that reaches boiling point would, in the hopes that someone would take me off the pressure cooker and help a sista become something more. I had burned out. I needed to retreat.

The first few months of 2016, saw a huge change in how I ran my life and my business. Not only did I pump the breaks, at times I think I bought it to a grounding halt. There were weeks where I didn't know what the hell I was doing, or if the spark would even come back. I just knew I had to allow myself to move through this gentle phase—believe that this was exactly where I was meant to be, and to feel exactly what I was meant to feel—while trusting the process along the way. That sounds *soooooo* much more glamorous than it actually felt.

A large part of the reason that I eventually made my way through came about in part by a release of judgment of myself and others. I committed to choose to see my life in a way that lifts me up, promotes fireworks and hugs my soul on every level. I started creating a life where there is a movement for an absence of judgment rather than living in the presence of a presiding judge, and I also stopped caring about what other people thought. That there, is a big one.

I pretty much had to just roll with it and hope that my juju came back.

Over the years, the seeker in me had gotten so caught up in the scope of *doing*, that I always had to be on my way to something.

I always had to have a *thing* in the works. A major goal, an activity or a big important focus. I thought this was an act of success and the mark of an incredibly productive person when in actual fact, I can now see it was driven by fear.

My New Year's resolutions read like a shopping list of things to tick off if you wish to be considered a successful human in your field. I took on every course I possibly could to better myself, which I now see was a sign of the fear of never actually *being* good enough.

If I wasn't always on the path, I felt like I would disappear and my relevance would diminish (whatever that means), and I would lose momentum. I got giddy off comments like, "I don't know how you do it all." I would rate my value and success based on the likes on a post and shares on my words. I constantly felt the pressure to keep climbing and succeeding and the whole thing was bloody exhausting. Part of me knows that I held on to a belief that if I was always moving forward, I would never have to look inwards because that was scary as hell, and another part of me just wanted to achieve it all so I could be *that* person.

At my most successful (busiest), even in my personal life, I wouldn't allow myself down time. Every spare minute of every day was filled creating and working. I constantly felt as if I was outside of my life hustling for my worthiness, just waiting to crack the code.

To get to that place where I had made it.

That space where everything fell into place and I had room and permission to enjoy what I created. I got that permission. Instead of waiting for some amazing being to say, "You've arrived," I decided to validate the crap out of myself.

It took a few months, but I am holding that permission slip in my journeyed and honest little hands. It is a sweet, sweet reality and one I solely created for myself.

**I don't actually have to DO anything.
I am everything I need,
when I choose to BE.**

Wooooooooah!

Right?

Upon releasing the need for approval, and stepping off the treadmill, I've found a myriad of new ways to validate and honor myself. Life has a simple splendor about it again, and the passion for creating stellar content and sharing this with you, and my clients, has returned, bolder and more profound than ever.

When I released the need to push, I allowed my energy to flow freely again and through that; I have found another layer to my truth, my new direction and some solid self-assurance. I don't know whether I released my grip on fear, or fear released its hold on me, but life is gentler, more peaceful and somehow it even feels softer.

If you have been feeling like you are striving, pushing and white knuckling it for a place within your life, I urge you to step back.

If you have been filling your days with expectations and are currently harboring the "Dis-Ease to Please," I urge you to turn inwards.

If you have been living your life in the fast lane, missing your moments and always looking towards the next big thing, then I would love you to stand still and release the need to fill the silence.

What I do know, is that fear wasn't put in front of us to pull us down. It wasn't put in front of us to keep us scared. It is there to keep us safe. It is put in front of us to give us an opportunity to learn from, to grow alongside and to figure out what we're made of within this spinning ball of dirt and water.

For me, it's also a part of my life to write about.

Fear is nothing more than a messenger and any moment we feel a negative emotion; we have the chance to create our own new beginning.

Gabrielle Bernstein works from *A Course in Miracles,* she calls every change in perception just that—a miracle. Every chance and every situation that we turn from fear or hate into light or love, is seen as a miracle.

Becoming Brave is about creating a life full of miracles, a life full of situations where we no longer turn away from fear. Instead we lean in and we *rise.*

**We rise up.
We rise up on our own.
We rise up with our sisters,
our friends, our family.
We rise strong
and we share the message.**

This doesn't need to mean that everyone needs to get up on stage, hold a microphone, be loud and take that route, that's not what I'm saying at all. There is a misconception as to what being *brave* and *bold* looks like and I'm-a-gonna set the record straight.

This book, these words, this message is actually about confidence.

Your confidence.

That trust in yourself and the willingness to breathe a little deeper and stretch a little further.

Confidence is a whisper.

It's a thousand tiny actions. It's a movement made in solitude and it's a decision only you can make.

Confidence is silent.

Fear, worry and insecurities are loud (pipe down, guys).

Confidence is a gentle knowing within yourself.

It's a trust in your ability to get it done.

It's assurance that you know you'll be OK regardless of how it works out—or not, even *knowing* that and still doing it anyway.

Confidence is badassery and bravery on a cellular level.

Confidence comes from self-assurance and that, lady friend, is a gift that only you can give.

That is how I am standing here today, but I'm still not immune to a fearful mutiny of my thoughts.

I was down in Melbourne, for a huge speaking gig and as I was walking through a tree-lined Melbourne park, I got thinking of how I had come to take these steps, on this path, in this park and it baffled me in the most beautiful of ways. I had to breakthrough my own fear based walls to get there and they had been appearing since the day I was offered the speaking event.

Fear is no stranger to a woman with an anxious mind like myself, but it never ceases to amaze me the different outfits she puts on to waltz on into my life as if she owns the place. It's almost as though she feels a new outfit, a new disguise, a brand-new situation and showing herself in an unfamiliar form will rattle me more.

She would be right.

Fear is at its scariest when you don't actually see it coming. If only our life came with theme music, so you knew that the shit was about to hit the fan, it certainly would give you the opportunity to prepare at least.

Fear can strike at any time and that's the beauty and mystery of it because you never know when she is going to pop up all sneaky like. She always arrives when you're minding your own business, and the next thing ... *boo!*

I'll paint a little picture for you.

There I was, at home, on the couch doing something laced with great significance at the time, I assure you (ahem ... Facebook). I had my writers outfit on, elastic pants all the way and I was rocking a mum bun like a boss and based on the way my boobs are sitting these days, I doubt I was wearing a bra. The baby had just gone to sleep as he was about ten-months-old at the time. I was crafting a post or something like that for my page which was nothing out of the ordinary as I love to get carried away in the process.

It was a very normal day just minding my own business.

Yes, there was coffee.

I was in my safe haven, doing all the things and this message popped up: "Hey Katie, what are you doing September and November? I've had a space open up at *Utopia*. It's yours if you want it."

- Floored.
- Instantly.
- Happy dance.
- I was electrified.
- I felt validated, seen and totally proud.

- **I was jazzed.**
- **A dream had come true.**
- **I had made it.**

My internal dialogue went a little like this: *This is freakin' fabulous. This is what I've been working towards. I get to deliver my message to women who get it. HOLY SHIT. This tour goes over three states ... three states! HOLY SHIT, this is a dream come true. Imagine how many epic women I'm going to get to meet.*

This lasted about seven seconds.

I thought a lot in those seven seconds.

Then just like clockwork *whooooosh* fear came like a wave: *Who am I to stand in front of these women? Who am I to tell my story? What is my story? Who is going to come and listen? What do I know about any of this stuff? How am I going to leave the baby? I can't do this. I can't travel to three states. I'm not ready. I positively can't do this because it's too big. It's too heavy. I'm not ready. This wasn't meant for me.*

Then I said, "Yes."

We are given two choices in the way that we look at everything in our life. For years, I felt there was only one and that was to listen to my thoughts. To live by my reactions. I assumed we were only ever given the option for one. I didn't realize that I could choose. I didn't realize that I had the power to be anything that I wanted to be and that I could choose the narration for my life's movie. I thought my thoughts were all there was. I didn't know I could make these thoughts work *for* me. I didn't know I could make my emotions work for me and I can't wait to teach you how to do the same, because my story is your story.

We all carry the same shit. We just put it in different packages.

Throughout this book, I won't just be sharing my stories, I will be sharing some stories of clients, friends and incredibly brave women who walk amongst you every day. We are all capable of brave moments.

We can all do hard things.

We are all capable of monumental triumphs and there is not one thing separating these women from you, we are all more alike than you realize.

One of the most damaging feelings and perspectives to carry in this world, is the view that you're alone.

You are never alone. I am going to use this book and everything it creates as a platform to introduce you to a mighty force of women who are moving through the same things.

Let's get started.

NEXT LEVEL IT

Let's dive on in. It's time to answer a few questions. I totes recommend journaling these out because clarity comes in the written word, but if you just want to mentally scribble away, do what feels right to you.

Where do you feel you have let FEAR take the wheel and steer your life?

What does BECOMING BRAVE look like to you?

Where have you seen yourself be **BOLD** within your life? Are you willing to enter into a contract with yourself and the women within this book?

Things that can be done *any* time—are rarely completed *any* time—I want things to be different from this day forward. You are entering a contract with your FEAR and you can gently whisper to her that the gig is up and you are turning the tables.

The vibe I want you to channel when writing up this little love bomb contract between you and the Universe, is the relationship you now wish to have with your Fear. It's also a great idea to acknowledge within here the past relationship the two of you shared. Become aware, and commit to the one you wish to honor moving forward.

Here's mine if you need a little kick-starter.

> *I, Katie Dean, on this day 7th April 2016, commit to a rocking new relationship with you, the FEAR. No longer will I allow you to dictate my decisions, to build walls around my visions or influence my behavior in a negative way.*
>
> *Moving forward, from this day, I am choosing to view you differently, acknowledge your presence in my life and give you credit where it's due. You will now and forever more be a sign post for growth, opportunity and a loving reminder of my ego wishing to keep me safe. I am a Queen. I can make decisions based on what I need and what's best for me, and while I will value your opinion, you will no longer be my navigator.*
>
> *I choose to let my soul be my compass and happiness my guide.*
>
> *Honestly, and with hand on heart sincerity,*
>
> *Kt.*

YOUR NEW CONTRACT WITH FEAR

I, _____ on this day, _____

commit to a rocking new relationship with you, the FEAR.

Honestly, and with hand on heart sincerity,

_____

Your
magnificence
and your
brilliance
on Earth
is in its
entirety
because
you are here
and you exist.

2

UNDERSTANDING THE F WORD

This FEAR factor gets a bad rap. I used to shy away from it, thinking that I needed to run from everything that scared me—yet, without this energy, this signal, this force field—we would more than likely be dead.

TRUE STORY

I shit you not.

There are so many different types of fear and throughout this book we are going to address a whole bunch of them because, well, quite frankly, I have been petrified of so many things at so many different times—and through my *really* anxious times—all of them at once.

For now; though, why is fear within us?

Why do we feel it?

Why is it part of our life?

In a nutshell, it is there to keep us safe. It's to stop us from walking into oncoming traffic. It's there to ward off danger such as falling off a cliff, or hanging out in dark alleys that hold a whole bunch of unforeseen nasties like robbers, spiders that fly, or land sharks (I know they're real).

Fear isn't all-bad; in fact, I think that fear can be a beautiful thing.

Thousands of years ago, when the biggest threat was random rogue apes and angry tigers, fear kept you and your Encino pals alive. Fear warned you and prepared you for a fight or flight response. If you were just minding your own business, making some arrows down by the river, no biggie, and suddenly you were in danger of being eaten, you sure as eggs are oval would want your body to signal you and say, "Hey Dorothy, you're not in Cansis anymore, you better get a wriggle on, or you'll soon to be lunch for this beasty."

FEAR SAVES LIVES

Thanks a bunch fear.

We owe you one.

The problem here though, is when fear becomes the driver of your life instead of a passenger. Fear can't be calling the shots. Fear doesn't deserve the power of navigator.

HELL TO THE NO

Fear is nothing more than a friend who can come along for the ride, who makes comments on the scenery occasionally, but has no real say in where you're going.

In this beautifully privileged day and age we live, we are always *on*. We are always contactable and there's often a lack of any white space. Space to just be. There's not a doubt in my mind that this is a massive contributor in our ability to process and handle our fear triggers.

Overwhelm is the new black for many creatives. Just in case you're saying that you aren't a creative, I'm actually talking about you. We all create in our own way. The big O usually rears its not so favorable head after there's been a stream of situations where you have gone against your soul's truest desire and your intuition. In doing so, you're saying "no to you" and "yes to *something* or *someone* else." With this little amount of down time, our brains rarely get a chance to unplug, to decompress, to slow down because there is always something to focus on and it's rarely the present. I've found that people are often scared to simply *be* with their thoughts, so their ability to process and make fair assessments of situations is tainted. The ability to go to our rational mind is diminished and the fight or flight response is triggered all too easily and so the cycle continues.

We are playing on our phone at the doctor's office.

We are at the doctors because our immunity has been compromised because we are so stressed all the time.

We are so stressed all the time because we are switched on 24/7.

We are switched on 24/7 thanks to our phones and technology encouraging that.

It's a pattern and we need to change it.

"Stressed out hot mess" looks terrible on me and I

wore it as a "badge of honor" for so long. I ran my day with my "busy banner" flying, fueled by coffee and the belief that this was how I had to function to get things done.

Pfffffft ... All lies.

I've proved that above theory wrong on every level.

When I was regional manager of Australia, for one of the biggest fitness companies, I was undoubtedly living a version of my dream life. I loved my job. I would wake at 4:00 a.m. every morning, check my phone right away and begin answering messages and emails from bed. I would then get up, make coffee and sit with my laptop checking off my to-do lists. I would relish in the quietness of dark and work until sunrise. I would then fit some exercise in and be back at the computer or training clients until 7:30 p.m., most nights. I loved my job and filled every waking minute working. I would have my phone by my side, seven or eight tabs open at once on my laptop—go from task to task without stopping—thinking I was doing the best job I could. I went from conference call to email, to meeting to face-to-face, and back again within the blink of an eye and felt guilty about taking lunch breaks.

To add to the fun of it all, I woke up one July morning, with this overwhelming urge followed by a confidence and clarity that I couldn't ignore. I was to start a blog and create a space that was nothing but real stories and positivity. A place to call my own and share my story with the world, or with no one, it really wasn't the point. **Your Wild Life** was born in 2013 and my trinity of platforms was created. A website, a Facebook page and Instagram were linked as a way for me to share all that I needed to process.

Spontaneity and serendipity working together to start a fire I hope never burns out.

When my son first arrived in April 2014, I knew that this pace couldn't continue. I knew I needed to slow it down. I knew I didn't want to live my life on fast forward. So, I resigned.

I decided to take *Your Wild Life* to the next level and I poured my heart and soul into my business. A business that could fit in around my life and not the other way around.

The way that I was spending my days changed dramatically with the arrival of a new bambino, but my beautifully capable and active mind did not. No longer was I connected to dozens of people at a time, solving problems, engaging in inspiring conversations and formulating plans around so many of the things that I was passionate about. Instead, it was usually me and a total bundle of love who hadn't yet learned to speak.

CONFRONTING

I was blessed with a mind that solves many problems at once and because I had trained my mind to function at such a capacity, the idea that now it was supposed to chill out and enjoy this new way of being wasn't meshing at all. I was introduced to my pal, Fear, on a whole new level and things definitely got worse before they got better.

Everything I had been running from and refused to acknowledge over the years was coming back up. All my shizzle, wild and free amongst all my shadows.

Dammit.

This time, I knew I couldn't run, literally—I had a baby on my boob—it was time to find a way through or die trying. Maybe a little less dramatic, or in hindsight that may in fact, be the magnitude of the way I was feeling because a life filled with fear of this kind is no fun at all.

I knew I was capable of so much more. I started to do the work. The real work with a real support system and my bullshit detector for myself set to sensitive. If I wasn't honoring what I needed I would be on it like a flash. I do believe, within this time frame, I met my soul for the first time. Until then, it was almost as if we'd had a virtual relationship. It was like I knew she was there. I would touch base with her regularly and sometimes daily for a quick chat. I'd followed her movements but we weren't actually connected, or in the same place at the same time—until we were and it was a much simpler and free flowing reunion than I'd ever hoped it could be.

My business and my platform became beautifully successful. I was writing for popular publications regularly, booking speaking gigs, and my coaching was booked out. It wasn't long before I fell back into my overachieving ways of the past. I was over-scheduling, overcommitting, overanalyzing and over-producing everything (this is what I was referring to as my boiling kettle moment in chapter one). Until, again, I got really honest with myself and shut it down. This time I knew the signals. This time I was aware of what was happening and how the fear was showing up. Let me tell you, the woman has some wily ways. She is a master of disguises and I promise we will cover a few of them later within these pages.

To help share what I was learning about myself and

how to fit in with this new world I had created, I decided to create an e-course. It was a project that helped me just as much as it has helped many of the women who've dared to look for another way.

My e-course, *Soulful Swagger*, had been a mind-blowing success in round one and it was now time to launch round two. *Soulful Swagger* looks at the twelve main elements in your life and is infused with tips and tools guiding you to live a real soulful inspired and free-flowing life, with confidence.

Exactly my kind of life vibe.

After launching round two of *Soulful Swagger*, I rebelled. I rebelled against the very system I had created. The system I had been an advocate for, the system I worked so hard to be a part of.

A full schedule. A social media time trap and the title of Successful Entrepreneur, according to what is portrayed in the media. I had ticked many of my big boxes, but I felt this deep desire and I couldn't ignore it any longer. I had this overwhelming urge, this undeniable need to unplug. I couldn't discount my mind and body calling to quieten the noise, to trim my life right back and open up the conversation with myself again.

My morning walks started to be carried out to the sound of nature. I wanted to hear the birds, hear the waves and tune in with my thoughts. Until now, I would play podcasts, listen to music, follow chakra cleanses and guided meditations, because I didn't want to be with my thoughts because this walk, after all, was a time for me to relax.

Sounds like something could be amiss, right?

Isn't silence supposed to bring you peace and calm?

Why would it be that silence causes me to feel anything but relaxed?

Isn't that what people do to tune off?

What was I frightened of?

I'll tell you what I was frightened of. That I would get myself to a place in my thought process that I couldn't come back from, or that I would follow a thought down a rabbit hole and take a full day to unravel the web of anxiousness I had woven for myself.

There had to be another way.

I know, I'm not alone in this now, but for a time I thought I was.

This was a pattern of avoidance I had had my whole life.

Avoidance. Denial. Busyness. Procrastination.

All fear.

Any of this sounding familiar, friend?

I had attempted to drink over it. Exercise over it. Travel away from it. Not talk about it. Work over it. All the while blaming my coffee, my situation, or someone else for my fearful ways.

We can never truly escape our thoughts.

We can of course, push them away for a time, pretend that hurts or situations never happened—that our feelings were never hurt—or that we had acted against our better judgment and hurt someone else in the process. We can attempt to push them down and numb them out, but they will always bubble back up to the surface, often at the most inopportune times. It can be a song on the radio, a smell, a name, a street sign and that's all it takes to bring up something we had wished we'd forgotten. It's human nature and unless you were taught how to deal and process these feelings and emotions properly in your youth, you can't be expected to know how to navigate them when you're wiser. That is of course, unless you seek it out or find yourself, like I did with no other choice because the waves were just getting too large. Truly a sink or swim moment amidst your very own perfect storm.

Our feelings and thoughts will keep coming up for us until we have essentially acknowledged them, honored them, felt them in their entirety and learnt from their existence. Awareness is the first key in any epic revamp of one's life, as Elizabeth Gilbert says, "I've never seen any life transformation that didn't begin with the person in question finally getting sick of their own bullshit."

And I was. So, I did.

Emotions are our own personal messengers and they only ever appear to tell you something. They're the gatekeepers to your deeper truth and there's nothing to be feared, and nothing to be avoided once you understand this. In fact, their whispers are our best anchors into a greater, more powerful language.

However friendly and well-meant these emotional couriers are, they are stories we choose to run from, scenarios that we want to avoid, and memories from days long gone that can haunt us in the wee hours of the morning, if we refuse to acknowledge them. This is where problems arise. If you don't choose to deal with these feelings as they surface, they will grow, amplify and often pick up momentum.

You can't run from them, work over them, party past them, or eat, sleep, repeat over them. The only way is to release something and allow it to pass. The only way through it is to move through.

TRUE STORY

If this is something that's new to you; it can feel huge, daunting and impossible to begin with. It almost feels counter intuitive—allowing yourself to feel worse, to feel better—but we are really only acknowledging what is waiting for us and what will take us to the next level.

The first step to making peace with your negative and not so welcome thoughts is embracing your ability to feel, shift and move through them by becoming aware of how each of these emotions appears within your body. Every emotion and every feeling comes with its own individual signal, both the great ones and the not so epic ones, but for today, let's focus on the feelings we naturally want to avoid:

- Fear
- Hurt
- Angst
- Doubt
- Worry
- Shame
- Disappointment.

The signals often show up as sweaty palms; a racing heart; tummy flips; a giddy head; a knot in your stomach, a lump in your throat ... the list goes on. Your signals of how these emotions feel is a blueprint unique to you and they are in fact, your personal delivery of a far greater message. The key to acknowledging your emotions is to stop running and figure out what that message really means and if it is true for you.

If you want to believe the way you're feeling; buy in and honor it and really get to know it. Or, if you wish after the personal inquiry discovering that feeling isn't right for you, flush it through the universal toilet and choose again.

The important thing is that you *really* ask yourself, and *really* honor what it is that's happening for you before you choose to respond rather than react. We must do our very best not to avoid, sugar coat or gloss over our feels.

If you're just sending an email, yet your feeling super scared and antsy, your fear switch could be a little trigger happy, or you could be about to be on the verge of a totally rad life changing application to something wonderful and only you can decide what's what.

Acknowledge, **Ask**, and **Proceed** with what feels right. It's OK for you to feel sad when something *sad* happens. Let it be and give yourself the space to feel it. Instead of thinking up ways to make it stop, start asking yourself, "What is going on here? Why am I feeling this way? What do I need to learn here?" Be open enough to listen and proceed with what feels right.

It's OK to feel depressed when life throws you curve balls and you go through a period of life-altering change. Understand that you're responding to what's going on in your world. This is OK. The sun will shine again.

It's OK to be really pissed off at someone that has hurt you. See them, or it for what it is, decide how you wish to proceed, then give it a flush. I've even been known to mimic the action of flushing a toilet upon processing my anger. Now, this might be a little crass but it really gets the point across and we are all friends, right?

You wouldn't leave your leftovers sitting in the toilet to fester and block up your pipes. You flush it. Do away with it out into the universal sewerage and then you can go on about your day. I can thank my beautiful kinesiologist for that analogy, although, I'm certain she was far more eloquent.

Allow yourself to feel what you need to feel until you don't need to feel that way anymore. Let it be OK. A lasting depression happens when we tend to have suppressed our emotions for far too long. To move through sadness and honor the reasons you are feeling low is a great big step in coming through—and again, when you're ready—simply doing the next right thing.

If you feel hurt—voice it, feel it, acknowledge it— then give yourself the space and time to come to a conclusion that feels right to you. When you are in pain, always know that you don't need to make a decision right now. In fact, the best decision you can make is to *not* make a decision at all.

Next Level It

Lost love and ended relationships with friends or partners can leave a hole in your heart, and a lump in your throat filled with all the words you wished you could have said, and the conversations that never happened.

The very best way to get closure when there is so much more left to say is to write. Write a letter. Write out your heart to the person who's occupying your thoughts and process all that needs to be said.

It might take one, it may take twenty.

You write until it's right.

Through a heartbreaking breakup in my early twenties, I think I wrote every night before bed for a month. Then it moved to once a week, then once every few weeks, until I no longer had anything left to say. Then when I had finally processed all I needed to process, I burnt all those letters because I knew I didn't need them anymore. The person I was writing them over didn't ever need to receive them. They were for me and for my peace. When someone will never give you what you need or crave, the bravest thing you can do is be the person who grants you permission to be and love yourself.

Take a look at the quote from the opening pages of this book again, and see what comes up for you now.

She wasn't looking for a knight, she was looking for a sword.

- Atticus

The point is that through the action of writing you are processing how you feel, and you are removing the emotions from a swirling vortex in your mind and returning that space to neutral territory. By doing so, you are creating a space where things can begin to make sense and you can begin to feel OK again.

Give yourself permission to feel how you need to feel, ride it out and look for the light. Your shadows are nothing to be feared because they can't last forever. When you are open to feeling "comfortable" with the "uncomfortable" you realize you can get through anything and a shadow will only ever appear when you, yourself, are blocking the light.

QUESTION TIME

Where in your life do you feel you have been masking or running from your emotions?

Why do you feel you are running from it?

What message is *really* trying to come through?

What are you going to do to honor it?

Acrnowledge

Ask

Proceed.

3

WHAT DID THAT SIGN SAY?

It's hard to differentiate between what's real and what's a reaction unless someone has explained and helped you connect with your signals. Every feeling, every emotion, every physical response doesn't necessarily always mean what you think.

Welcome to the world of signals.

It's no secret that I have a busy mind and a loud and somewhat offensive ego. My programmed response naturally is to get anxious and start to overthink all the things, so learning how to work with that; play with it and take it out for a spin, day after day has been quite the journey.

When I realized that my ego and fear were actually there to keep me safe, things began to soften and I began to understand and respond rather than react.

Somewhere along the line, I had simply gotten a little trigger happy with my *Uh-Oh* radar and accepted the snowball effect as my normal. Once I was aware of my thought process, my ego, and how they worked together, I could slowly start to get her on side, or at least, understand what was really going on. See, these emotions and these feels, the fearful or hectic energy, can't hurt us, they're just signals. They're nothing more than a reaction to a thought, or a situation you are experiencing in that moment.

If the *fear* comes up and there is nary a bear in sight, understand it for what it is. You don't have to buy into the feeling. You *can* choose another way, the story that follows the signal is up to you and you *can* choose not to judge.

**The fear is just a signal.
You get to control the story.**

Wild, right?

It's important we understand emotions and energy for what they are and allow ourselves to move through them. Any emotional response can only last for around ninety seconds, until we buy in and carry it on through our trajectory of fearful thoughts. This is an actual scientific fact, discovered by Dr. Jill Bolte Taylor, who found that even the strongest emotional trigger can only last for ninety seconds until we then choose to carry it on.

The power lies in how we choose to respond to fear and these heavy emotions that come our way. As they are just energy, we need to allow them to pass through with a simple acknowledgement and avoid deeming them good or bad. When we label any situation as good or bad, positive or negative, we immediately trigger another set of emotional responses and so the cycle continues.

If you choose to avoid or even worse, suppress these emotions, *that* is when things build up and often show themselves in a far more physically damaging and emotionally challenging way. Think stomach ulcers, depression, addiction, hair loss, eating disorders, severe anxiety ... I could go on, but I think you catch my drift. When we become aware of our thoughts, we become aware of the signals that feeling fearful ignites within our body and we can then make a choice that will serve us long term.

When I move from my most conscious self, into my fearful ego-state and my mind wants to run away with me, I get this wave. It's like a head to toe fearful wash and my tummy flips as if I were in an elevator. I can get hot. I get racy and there's a feeling of dread or panic. This all happens in the space of around two to three seconds.

This is my sign.

It's pretty much my version of the bat signal.

It's where I get a chance to get all Ninja like with my emotions because all of this is done in secret. You wouldn't even know that I am riding the waves and about to snap to action like a lady boss. #Badass

That signal I just described used to mean: *Woman, get the fuck out of here, because shit is about to hit the fan,* closely followed by, *you can't do the thing, who are you to attempt this anyway—they don't like you, they never liked you—you're going to make a fool of yourself. Retreat, go back, go hide, do not pass go, and never attempt anything like this again—ever.*

Quite the *convo*, right?

No wonder I used to panic and retreat. No wonder I didn't feel secure in social situations unless I had a drink in my hand. I certainly wasn't doing myself any favors with the epic *pump up* speech I'd give myself at every opportunity. The thing is though, all those nasty comments I'd tell myself were just stories. The *fear trigger* was way off. I was always safe, but I was often faced with an opportunity to grow, to be a little more confident and to learn something about the world, or myself, and that's what would initiate the spiral.

Our ego hates growth. Our ego hates any sort of evolution of our consciousness so she does her best to keep us in a box. #Whatasport

The great news is **YOU hold the power**.

Once you are wise to her jibe you can change the meaning to the signals. You can interrupt the program, you can flip it on its head and *that* is where the magic happens.

I still remember the day it hit me. This signal didn't mean what I thought it meant all along. This fear; this dread, this doubt didn't mean the stories I was telling myself. I had been reading the signals wrong all this time.

Imagine if Batman, Batwoman, or Bat-gender-neutral-person went on a fearful vendetta every time the signal was raised. Gotham would be in all sorts of strife.

What if, like the bat signal, my fear didn't mean turn away and run, it meant lean in and rise? I'll say that again.

What if your fear didn't mean turn away and run, it meant lean in and rise?

Holy shit. Can you feel that? The winds of change just blew your hair back.

What if every fearful situation was a chance for you to be brave?

Suddenly, the weather changes and the world looks a whole lot different.

This doesn't only apply to fear though, my friend. Have you ever thought about what the other emotions are really telling you about yourself, and the situation you're in, in that moment?

EMOTIONS ARE MESSENGERS

Think about so many instances that you find yourself in day to day. Some of them are stressful and really full on, and I have no doubt you are just doing your darndest.

It's OK to feel scared sometimes.

It's OK to feel depressed if something heavy has just happened in your life. It's your body, mind, and soul responding to an event and it's totally OK to not feel OK all the time.

I am a massive advocate for allowing yourself to feel all your feelings and not judge any of them because they each have something to say, and who are we to judge that?

Let's take a walk and look at a few of the big shots of the emotional world.

Anger: Where there's anger, there's passion. Its presence is usually an indication that your expectations haven't been met and of course, that shit will make you angry. Anger can also be Sad's bodyguard, so instead of facing the disappointment, we get our rage on.

Anxiety: The micro-manager of emotions, usually comes about when we try to control and predict every possible scenario, situation and outcome. The ultimate *over* analyzer is always an indication that you are either future trippin', or dwelling on days long gone. It's there for a reason and perhaps that's to let you know it's time to come back to your now.

Sadness: Celebrate the fact that you feel and you care. That you feel something so deeply that it can't help but change your energy—sadness proves that you *loved*—and that is something worth it all.

Happiness: Pure joy is deserved by all. Feeling this energizing emotion shows that you are in your present, that you are operating from a place of love, and that you are energetically clear. All hail the happy vibes.

Regret: You tried for something and that is far better than all the *what-ifs*. Acceptance and compassion are key to moving through regret and allowing regret to be a symbol of how much you've grown. You can't hold yourself to a standard of grace you didn't hold at the time. Forgive yourself for not knowing what you do now and move the F— on.

Frustration: A symbol of a communication breakdown. A block of some sort. Where there's smoke there's fire, and some honest self-inquiry will allow you to pinpoint what the real underlying issue is. It's never about the spilt milk, so save yourself another argument and address the issue you've been avoiding.

Contentment: A love and appreciation for your present

moment. *Naaaaaaaw.* How freakin' rad. Let's all aim for that, shall we?

Surprise: When something has beautifully exceeded your expectations.

Envy and comparison: What a useless use of energy comparison is. Comparison is a sign that you've taken your eyes off your own lane. It shows itself when you start to devalue yourself and question your worth.

DON'T DO THAT

Comparison is TRULY the thief of all happiness and solves no other purpose other than to diminish your NOW.

DON'T.
Do.
That.

The list goes on, and I'm so glad it does.

Feeling our feelings should come naturally, but for many of us, we have to unlearn so much of the programming of years gone by. For some reason, society has us believing that it's *not* OK to not feel OK. This is horseshit.

More often, than not, we are programmed to run away from the painful, cultivating the need to fix the uncomfortable and the necessity to put on a brave face when the shit hits the fan.

No.

No, thank you.

Pass.

There are times in life where it's going to be hard and it's OK to struggle. There are times in life where we are going to go through depressing situations and it's hard to do so without feeling depressed. There are times in life where we are going to be under an immense amount of pressure, and to feel the effects of that are totally normal and OK.

It's completely acceptable to have low vibe times. To feel the loss of loved ones, a breakdown of relationships, or change in careers, they are all going to evoke an emotional reaction within you. You are not a freakin' robot, lady. If you prick your finger, you bleed, so show yourself some compassion in the tumultuous times and know that this too, shall pass.

Just like Earth has her seasons, so do we, and they each deserve respect and space. Whenever I have allowed myself the space to go through whatever it is that I'm going through, something beautiful has come out the other side. A new wave of creativity, a better understanding of who I am, as a person, or a complete reframe and new direction of my life's path. Pure magic. The times that I have bottled it up, pushed it aside, or attempted to drown it out are the times where the issues stay with me a lot longer.

Pushing through the low vibe times didn't get me through them quicker, it just added a layer of frustration to an already shitty situation. Your emotions are energy and symptoms of something much larger at play, the "well of your soul" runs deep, young one. They are beautiful powerful messengers and it's time to start asking the question, "What am I REALLY feeling?" And, be OK with whatever comes up.

NEXT LEVEL IT

KNOW YOUR SIGNALS

It's time to truly get amongst it. This is the work you will be doing your entire life, but this may be the first time you are putting it all out there for REAL! I want you to do some free writing. You can either do your free writing here or in your own special place (I suggest your own special place because girl, you're *gonna* need more room). Wherever **feels** right for **you**.

What comes up for me when I feel **fear**?

What are my triggers? The instances that usually set me off.

How does my body feel when I experience doubt, fear, dread, anxiety, and where do I feel?

How does it feel when I feel **happiness**?

What are the things in my life that bring about my **true** happiness?

How does it **feel** in my body when I am **happy** and at **peace**?

Now, there you have it, lovely lady. Can you see the difference between operating from a loving centered and calm place, and from a fearful, impulsive place?

Now, you can see when the **ego** is taking over, and you can now choose happiness over fear any time you feel it creep in.

You have the ability to *always* choose again. You now know what it feels like when the ego pops up and you can turn on the lights quick smart now. You have just become aware of the early signs and this is powerful information. You have the tools. You can see the difference and you never have to feel imprisoned by your thoughts or feelings again.

CAN I GET A HELL YEAH?

If you want to know more about each of your emotions and how they show up for you, do some free writing on them also. You may be surprised with what you uncover.

Your Fear
is a chance
for you to
be brave.

4

EVERY THOUGHT IS A CHOICE

W e have sixty to seventy thousand thoughts a day. A day. *Gasssssp!*

Now, I bet you're thinking that's a whole bunch of options for rocking an inspired and positive life, right? *ABSO-FREAKEN-LUTELY.* If you choose to use them that way, of course. I was shocked when I heard this number initially, this escalated even more when I found out that most of these thoughts are the same. Have you ever actually become a witness to your thoughts? Have you ever actually decided to pay attention to the narration you are giving your life's movie? The notion that our thoughts really do create our world is nothing new, right? You are probably aware that the content of your gorgeous melon has a direct effect on the way you live your life. In fact, your external world is usually a reflection of how your mind is travelling. You could be in the biggest shit storm of your life, but remain cool, calm and collected because you are in that place mentally, or you could be in your bed at night, physically safe but your mind is creating a vibe for you something akin to the scenes from the movie, *War Horse.*

Perception is everything.

What we aren't all aware of is that there is a choice for every thought we think and the responses we choose to have. I certainly wasn't aware. I thought my shitty mood was real. I thought when I was anxious that I had to wear that. I thought that when I was fearful it was because whatever the situation I was in, was in fact, horrifying. I had no idea about the power of perception. Our ability to choose our thoughts and the flow on effect that these decisions would have on our life.

I now understand a very important fact.

All thoughts are real, but not all thoughts are true.

We get to choose the stories we decide to take on as our truth. I now know, that we can reprogram our entire thought process simply by becoming aware.

Awareness is the first step in any real shift.

Becoming aware is the gateway to real change.

Awareness is absolutely essential in order to bring the *scaries* over to your side of the table.

We want to befriend the F-Bomb.

We want to disarm both angst and our ego, and the first step is realizing when your inner mean girl is up to no good. It's a powerful moment when you catch your ego early in action and have the ability to switch gears and change perceptions, which actually means, you change your reality.

It's your own sort of magic and I'm totally down for believing we each have a little witch in us.

As Rebecca Campbell says, "We are the granddaughters of the witches they couldn't burn."

SO EPIC!

There is always a physical trigger when it comes to crossing over from a loving state to a fearful perspective. By knowing how these feelings show up for us and how they feel in our bodies, we can choose to respond rather than be swept along emotionally.

My triggers can vary, depending on what's happening in my life. It really is fairly generalized with me, and my worries can attach to anything. Especially, if I haven't been conscious of creating space in my day for me to honor my needs. I will say this though, I'm fabulous at future tripping and there's always room for some gnarly self-shaming and if it were a valued skill, I would consider myself an expert. **Self-shaming** when you break it down is the shaming of one's **self** ... how *freakin' brutal.*

Why do we feel it's OK to get all high and mighty with ourselves? We can be so cruel. The judgment police. I have had myself positioned so out of reach at times in my life. All the way up there on my high horse, judging part of myself, mind you, that I would have had to tuck-and-roll to get down. We have the right to do almost anything in this life, but we don't have the right or the authority to turn on ourselves, yet so often we do.

Once I figured out what my internal signals were, I gained the upper hand. It wasn't instantaneous. It wasn't some miraculous quick fix, but it is becoming less of a burden and more of a call to action. Now, whenever I feel my bat signal, I lean in. Instead of running, I rise. Instead of cowering, I tango. Instead of waiting for the storm to pass, I grab a brolly and search for the sunshine.

You *can* play with your fear because every thought is a choice. You *can* choose to be led by your ego or walk with your intuition.

Do you know the difference? You can tell who's leading the march by the way it feels within your body. How do you do that? It's coming back into yourself again, honing in on that awareness, embracing that first shift.

We always know which way to go, we *always* know what's right for us, sometimes however, we lack the trust to embrace that feeling enough to allow it to do its job and guide us. When my ego is leading the charge, I feel insecure, I feel scared and I feel small. I am unsure of myself, I need reassurance and I feel uneasy. I feel unworthy and often lost. I get frustrated and am quick to anger. When my intuition is leading the way, I feel secure. I feel light and I feel relief. I am operating from a place of loving trust and I feel spacious. Anything is possible in this space because anything IS possible.

It's normal for the two to grapple often, and initially, every time there is a quiet moment, or a fork in the road of some kind. Ultimately in this life, in each situation, a decision about who you are going to follow—intuition versus ego—will need to be made. The fear about making the wrong choice rears its confusing head, but I want to propose a question to you.

What if there is no wrong?

What if we took the notion that there is a **right** way and a **wrong** way off the table?

What if there were only choices?

Ponder this for a moment because this line of thinking set me free.

Knowing this is a GAME CHANGER.

It set me free of the hectic judgment I put on myself. It set me free of the pressure to be perfect. It also set me free from the lame ass stories I was living through and carrying with me over the mistakes I have made in my lifetime.

Recently, i made a ballsy move to listen to my intuition over my ego and it was one of those moments where I distinctively had a dalliance with both the light and the dark parts of myself. Almost every woman, I know, has a connection with her hair. Some more than others, but we all know the power of a good hair day, and the equally familiar wish for the ground to open up and swallow us whole on the days where your locks just don't cut the mustard. In all seriousness, I know that a conversation about hair may seem trivial after some of the epic truths shared throughout this book, but I hid behind my hair for many years, so stay with me.

I was nicknamed, Boofhead in my high school years, and bullied *heavily* for this wildly curly hair I used to brush to try and fit in. I would cry most afternoons and begged my parents to change schools. I didn't look like the other girls, I didn't feel accepted and I was all so very awkward. I formed this limiting belief that I needed to have long blonde hair to feel beautiful. I desperately tried to grow it for thirteen years, but due to the different medications I was on it never really grew, or if it did, it snapped off quite early. I wore countless sets of hair extensions, and a large part of my self-worth was wrapped up in other people's perceptions of this look I tried so hard to cultivate for myself. I never felt enough. I was very aware of this superficial need to feel pretty, and that I had created the notion that my hair was the secret to being beautiful. As I grew and as I began to change my life, I really started to work on this, and what this false perception of self was doing to me and the way I showed up in this world. When my son was born, I decided enough was enough. I didn't want to be the woman who hid behind her hair, who didn't believe in herself, or whose value and self-worth relied upon something external. I was so much more than that, so I got rid of the extensions. That was my first bold move stepping a little closer to the edge. Due to the years of over styling and under loving my hair, it was a real mess. I cruised around for a year or so with it in a messy bun, pretty much still hiding, but in a different sort of way until I was at my hairdressers in September of 2015, and I said, "Cut it, cut it all off."

You could have heard a pin drop.

Unsure of what I was actually asking, Leisa my beautiful hairdresser and friend gently questioned me, knowing full well of the attachment I had to my hair. Immediately the internal conversation erupted: *You can't do that? You can't cut your hair, what will Brendan say? What will everyone else say? You have to speak in front of hundreds of people next month. You couldn't possibly cut your hair.*

I felt small. Shy. Afraid and ashamed. Gutless even.

So, I was going to leave it and reneged on my suggestion. Immediately, though, on voicing this change of heart I felt sad. I knew there was more, I knew that the verbal vomit that had intermittently just poured out was my ego and there was more to be said.

My intuition piped up. My inner guide. My internal GPS.

There was another voice: *You can do this. You are so much more than your hair. You deserve a change. Set yourself free. Who cares what anyone thinks. F THAT! F THEM! BE. YOU. BRAVELY.*

The more I listened, the louder this little voice got and I instantly grew taller in my chair.

I felt stronger. Empowered. Sure of myself. I felt so sassy that I knew I was on the right path. So, there in that beautiful black leather chair under all those lights I said, "Cut it." And she did. It was the best decision I could have made for myself. I set myself free. I knew the signals and I turned the game on itself. This was so much more than a haircut, it was me taking power back over my life.

Will, I grow my hair again? Yeah, I'd say so but it won't be to hide behind. It will be because I like to try new things and experiment with new looks perhaps, but it will never be to avoid myself and fit a mold I create in my mind. I will tell you this though, every time I have gone against my intuition the shit has hit the fan. Not literally, because that is a mess I would never want to clean up, but all my biggest lessons have come from not listening to that little voice, that gut feeling and that inner guide. This does nothing more than solidify my standing on the theory that there is no wrong when it comes to decisions, only choices. Whenever I have tried to override the system and ignore my intuition it usually comes back in the form of a lesson, which then leads to a better understanding of who I am as a person—what I believe in, where my moral compass sits—and how I want to live my life. Lessons make us wiser, they help us expand. So really, the fear around making a mistake drops away when you know you will be gifted with a lesson if the outcome you receive isn't in fact, what you had hoped. Lessons can never be wrong.

Can you see now that you win no matter what the outcome?

The power of perception is a beautiful thing.

"When we change the way we look at things, the things we look at change."
—Dr. Wayne Dyer

The dialogue and the story that we attach to every situation is entirely within our control. If the way you are choosing to see an event, a situation, a relationship, or an issue currently doesn't serve you, change it. You have the power to decide to see things in a new light. A simple question to ask yourself is, "How can I see this differently?" A question that can make all the difference.

For instance, right now, as I'm writing this, it's 5:20 a.m. and my husband comes out and declares that he may as well go to the gym. I haven't had a chance to go to the gym this whole week because of his work schedule and I thought I had my window at 6:00 a.m., you could cut the air with a knife. He does have to work today, but I also have Archer, and that time to myself to train does wonders, but having the argument this morning back and forth over who deserves it more, is exhausting and I am just not up for it. My initial perception is one of anger, resentment and frustration, and I feel that in my tummy and my entire body. It doesn't feel good. I don't like it and it's not serving me at all. It's certainly not affecting him in the slightest, as he stands there slurping on his hot coffee looking all smug (why do men do that?).

I'm going to change it. How can I choose to see this differently? As soon as I finish this chapter and have breakfast, I'll go put on my exercise gear, and take Archer down to the oval and we can have a run around and a play. WIN. WIN.

There is always a way through every block, you just have to be willing to lay your weapons down, lean in to that discomfort, look for the positive and choose a better way. Getting out of my head and into my body afforded me the opportunity to change my perception of my situation and choose my perspective. I know my triggers. I know what fear feels like and I know that there is another way. The brave and bold move in this instance was to find a new way to look at things and lean in to the signals. It was in fact, the bravest move to lose the victim mentality, choose to see things differently and act accordingly, and all of this came about because I was aware. So freaken simple, yet oh, so, effective.

NEXT LEVEL IT

Where in your life, in this very moment, can you play with your perception?

How can "I" choose to see this another way? See what comes up for you.

You may just surprise yourself, and who doesn't love a surprise?

There are
only ever
choices.
Please *choose*
you.

5

FEAR IS A CHAMELEON

Fear is a Chameleon—she can take on many forms—she is a temptress, a sneak, your best friend and she also has a foul mouth. Maybe that's just my fear wench, she tends to drop the F-bomb like a sailor on leave.

Fear is everywhere and shows up for us wearing a whole bunch of different hats. We call it by a myriad of different names because somehow that makes us feel better about ourselves, right? Because someone once told you that it's not so badass to be scared, right? WRONG!

Being scared means you are trying for something, that you are daring to go where you haven't gone before. Feeling fear is totally normal and if you never had a little angst in your life, I would say you are getting pretty cozy in your comfy beige box. While there is absolutely nothing wrong with the comfort zone and hanging out here between big life events, feeling fear with friends, however you want to look at it is badassery on another level. Being the shape shifter that fear is, I thought, for your viewing pleasure today, we will break a few of those down so you can see if these not so cool kids show up in your world.

Firstly, let's look at **perfectionsim**.

Perfectionism is really just a dressed-up word for fear. It's fear with more letters. It's a pig in lipstick, so let's just call it what it is, Fancy Fear. It masquerades as a highly desirable skill, but really the underlying vibe is that you are afraid of falling short—of being judged, of not being perfect, of having flaws, of being seen—and my personal favorite, a fear of succeeding. Perfectionism will keep you from ever releasing your GOLD. It keeps you tweaking, shuffling and recalibrating. Perfection keeps you stagnant, wearing self-doubt for a cardigan yet you insist on calling it a sweater. It is what it is and it's time to face the music.

Embrace your first pancake. The first one is never quite right, it has all the makings of a beautiful meal, but the pan may be cold, it looks a little off, you burn the edges, or it could be a little runny. You can add berries, smoother it in syrup, throw some nuts on it to try and make it better—but at some point, you just have to say, "Fu%k it, I'm hungry and serve it up." The first pancake does not dictate your life's meal. It's not your destination, it's just the first stop, so let it be perfect in its imperfections.

If this isn't your first rodeo, then let's look at things a different way.

What is the worst that can happen if you *do* the thing?

What is the worst possible situation that could arise from you *not* doing the thing?

I feel that living with regret over not bringing your

dream to life creates way more of a sucky vacuum effect within your existence. Take some time for a little self-enquiry and examine what is the real reason you need everything to be completely perfect?

How does that feel to you?

Is that something you want to live with?

Is that a truth you want to wear?

You can decide that here is where the journey begins and it's time to launch forward. You don't have to pen the greatest book ever written, if you have a story to tell, let that be your story. You don't have to give the best audition that the world has ever seen, you just have to get on stage and shine. What happens next is irrelevant. You don't have to cook the best freakin' meal anyone has ever cooked, you just have to ensure that no one goes hungry. Choose what your mission is—get clear on that—and let's not give it any more power than the actual act itself.

I wrestled with perfectionism myself for quite some time. Let's just say I'm in remission. Loosely.

When I created *Soulful Swagger*, my first and most loved up e-course, I was so afraid of it not being perfect that it held me back for so long. I knew I had to create this e-course—she was persistently knocking at my door—not too different from this crazy gem. I knew I had to get it out into the world, I had spent so long on the content and I couldn't get my head around the way I wanted her to look, eventually I just pointed and said, "that one" when it came to the logo's. I knew that if I didn't I would be a slave to perfection forever. The first round didn't have to be seamless, it just had to work. It had to give the results, it had to be my truth, what I know to be helpful and effective and it had to leave people feeling better than they came. I knew my *why*, and my why was wrapped in my message. That was my first step; nothing more, nothing less. That was my first pancake and what a freakin' tasty treat she was. The results were just as I'd hoped. They bought me time to go back to my beautiful project and give her the look I knew she deserved. Had I waited, had I stalled, had I let fear hold me back of getting it right, there may not have been a round two. There may not have been a round one, but there would have been a lot of unrest and unfinished business, and that, I don't have time for.

**Where is the BRAVE for you
in releasing control?**

FEAR OF BEING SEEN

The fear of being seen as you see yourself.

The fear of being seen as a fraud.

The fear of being judged even half as harshly as you judge yourself.

Heavy freakin' load dude. *Woah.*

This one is crazy big. If you have ever shied away from being you, or allowing all of you to come through, then this my friends is your Everest. This one got me good.

There have been plenty of moments where I rubbed up against the need to be perfect and the fact that I'm not has done me in. I am so far removed from what would be considered by many to be perfect that it now makes me chuckle. I have held such judgment of myself over my youth and the way I navigated that super sensitive, totally confusing time which was in fact, with all the grace of a bull in a china shop. I've had to do *such* work on myself, to be OK with the gray area's and to get to a place where I now understand that I am who I am, because of the path I've taken.

For many moons, it was almost as though I was shuffling around my life carrying a badge of dishonor for every perceived slight I have ever made in my life. I would rehash over every wrong turn; conversations that could have gone better, relationships that should have ended long before, doors and calls that should have been left unopened or unanswered and nights where I probably should have just stayed home. My less than shiny moments were all pivoting points. They were all moments that allowed me to grow, to choose again, to forge another path, and because they weren't perfect, they have given me stronger morals, a more certain sense of self and a stronger belief in the powers of my intuition. More so, exactly what sort of things can go wrong when I attempt to silence my inner knowing, and go the other way. Not having walked a perfectly straight line should never be the precipice for staying still. My sense of self will no longer be based on someone else's perception of who I am, and in that simple revelation, I found my BRAVE. I want to stand and shout and say what I'm thinking. I want to learn and grow and expand my views on everything that interests me. I want to give myself all the love and support I can, because I freakin' deserve that and so do you. What matters most is that your heart is true and it's about who you are today. You don't need to hold yourself accountable to a truth you no longer believe about yourself, and anyone who chooses to judge you for when you were at your most vulnerable, sure as hell doesn't deserve to be around you as you shine. There is such freedom that comes in owning your place, in your story and standing tall for all to see. You are the perfect compilation of every experience you have ever had up until this point, and that is both beautifully chaotic and magical in all its complicated simplicity. Allow yourself to be just that. Just as you are. All that you need to be.

Where can you step up, step out and step into your brave?

Are you in the spiritual closet?

Do you find yourself secretly mesmerized by the moon cycles?

Do you love self-improvement books, but never discuss them with your friends?

Do you have a love affair with crystals, sage your home, get giddy at the faintest whiff of Nag Champa, but keep this almighty goodness to yourself?

If you were smiling and nodding along to any of those questions, then you, sweet Sista, may be in the spiritual closet, and guess what, I have only recently been brave enough to venture out a little more. I wouldn't say I'm a very religious person, but I am deeply spiritual in the way I live my life. I use signs, vibes and feelings to make my life's decisions. I run my business based on what feels best at the time, and I use my breath as an anchor to bring me back to my safe space on this wide and wild Earth. I know I am supported and I trust that what's meant for me won't ever pass me by.

Do I ever have "poor me" moments? Hell yes, but

I don't wallow in the shadows for anywhere near as long, as I used to. Do I share my love of crystals with everyone, and feel comfortable to sit down at a table filled with strangers and announce that, "I'm going to smudge my house this afternoon?" No, I haven't so far, but it doesn't mean I wouldn't. It's not feeling so witchy to me anymore.

I've started to let go of the need to be understood, and now am on a quest to understand.

Part of the reason I think I kept a special part of my life away from others is because I was worried that I would be ridiculed, misunderstood or judged. I don't necessarily think this was a mistake because not everyone is going to understand your energy, not everyone is going to vibe on the same frequency, and not everyone will get excited about what moves you, but they don't have to. Only you need to be OK with where you are and what means something to you.

How do you know what to share and what to keep private? Only share that with the world that you have totally and unequivocally accepted, understood and processed yourself. If you are still a little unsure about something and are cautiously enjoying the discovery, don't put the added pressure on yourself of needing validation from someone else. This beautiful adventure that you're embarking on is not meant for them, it's meant for you.

People can also be very fearful of what they don't understand. Things can get said that sting, so unless you are fully firm in your truth and can't be wavered by outside opinions, keep your treasure to yourself until the time that you are. Not everything *needs* to be for everybody. On the flip side, if you are ready, there's such freedom and bliss in sharing your beliefs and loves with the world. Stepping into yourself and owning your passions, curiosities and loves, allows the world to see who you really are. Living your most beautiful unique and loved up life gives those around you permission to do the same. This doesn't only apply to spirituality. This applies to different passions, beautiful hobbies, health regime's, or the desire to take the plunge into those bigger things. Whatever closet you're hiding in, whatever you're shielding from the world, the day that you are ready to share it, I can't wait to hear about it. If you're bursting at the seams to share your passion but still fear the judgment of others, find someone who vibes the same way, start a conversation and begin there. The world needs more people who are alive in their uniqueness and celebrating their love for whatever it is that brings them joy. The best way to feel accepted is to start by accepting yourself. It's the best club you'll ever belong to.

The only approval that's needed is your own.

Fear of Failure

What if failure is not what you think? I'm not sure I believe in the text book definition of failure. Let's take a little look just to double check.

Failure - noun: According to the jolly peeps at *Oxford Dictionary* they define failure as, "not successful, a lack of success in doing or achieving something, opposite success, not doing something."

Well friends at *Oxford*, I am not so sure about your choice of words here, and I am most certainly not picking up what you are putting down. I am not willing to roll with your vibe, actually, I am *totes* against it. The only way to truly fail at something, I believe, is to never give it a go. That is where the disappointment lies. That's where there is no sense of achievement. The success could never be there because you never believed in yourself enough to try. That is true failure because you, and only then, let your dream and inspiration fail you. Let's dive into this a little more.

So, your business closes. Did you fail? No, you just shut down. You had a red-hot go and perhaps it wasn't your time or some elements weren't quite right.

Did you have fun? Did you follow your passion? Did you learn anything about yourself and your industry? Then power to you, party person, that's epic. Not every passion is meant to be a business; therefore, the pressure that you put on your passion when you ask it to earn you money is huge. What if your passion was meant for you and you only? What if, you were given a love of something so great that its only role in this world was to bring you joy? HOLY. SHITBALLS. That's not failure, that's not defeat, learning *that* is a victory and now you get to enjoy your thing without the pressure of having it keep your power switched on.

So, your relationship ends. Did you fail? No. Every relationship has a beginning, a middle and an end. Someone leaves or someone dies. Harsh, but true. Perhaps you learnt all you could from your dalliance with this heart. Perhaps you walked as far as you were meant to with this soul. Not everything is meant to last a lifetime, appreciate it for what it was, what it taught you. Let it be at that.

The only way to truly fail is to be too scared to face up to your true potential. That my friends, is failing you.

FEAR OF JUDGEMENT

"What Susie says about Sally, says more of Susie than of Sally."

Quick, someone put that on a bumper sticker. Oh, wait ... while this is a legit fear, I almost don't want to give it any air time in this heart space of ours because there are two parts to it. One of which we can't control; we can't control what someone else thinks of us. We can't control what someone else's perception of us are, nor should we ever attempt to try. What a waste of energy. There are far more epic life goals to be journeyed towards than the desire to be liked. Say you decided to enter a cooking competition. You made the most beautiful gourmet chicken burger. Seriously, off the charts delicious, you had fancy lettuce, melted fancy cheese and you even used fancy pants fresh organic micro herbs. Then the judging comes. Time to present your masterpiece, deep breaths, you've never met the judges before and you placed it in front of a vegan. Now, she is not going to love your burger. She is not even going to like it. She is probably going to think it's the worst burger she has ever seen, and that is because to her, it quite possibly is. Now, if you based your self-worth and your cooking skills on the opinion of someone else, then you are up for one hell of a hard road.

Living to seek the approval of others is like waiting for a permission slip to go to the bathroom. It might work

77

for a while, but eventually you are going to be seeking, no one will be there to gratify your obvious need and you might just shit yourself. Figuratively, and literally. What a mess.

Your sense of self should never be wrapped up in someone else's perception of you.

Who knows what path they have walked in their lifetime. Who knows what side of the bed they got out on, if they were hugged as a child, or if they even like your hair color, because sometimes, that may actually be what they base their opinion on. Who knows? Quite frankly, it's none of our business.

Second part of this judgment vibe. When you love yourself enough, it means being OK with all the not so shiny bits of your makeup. When your actions and life path are motivated from a place of love for what you're doing, rather than seeking outside approval, then the fear of being judged loosens its grip on you. I have wrestled with this one myself, and from time-to-time it always ends up with me throwing my hands in the air and shouting, "F-IT" and doing it anyway.

When I put myself out into the world openly and speak from my heart, there is always going to be someone, who is triggered by something I say. What I mean by triggered is that I voice something that hits a nerve for them, that ruffles their feathers, that they aren't ready to hear and they will get defensive and decide to judge me for it. I often have rubbed shoulders with the fact, that I, have had a bumpy ride. I went through my own stuff. I have my own fair set of regrets, but without my regrets, I wouldn't have my lessons. Without my lessons, I wouldn't have my growth, and without my growth, I would still be an eighteen-year-old, lonely girl swimming around in a blurry haze of waiting for Friday's and cheap spirits.

I have worked hard to become the woman I am today. I had to build myself up, unlearn so much that I had told myself about who I was, and got back to the core of who I am, and that makes me a maverick.

The way that someone treats you is more a reflection of the relationship they have with themselves than an accurate reflection of you.

END SCENE.

Fear of Missing Out (*FOMO*)

Picture this. You have your weekend planned out. A weekend of YOU. All your favorite things are included, some creative time, exercise is in there, maybe you'll binge watch your favorite TV show, a trip to the markets and even a little food prep to help set you up for an amazing week. Then, you see via a group text message that there is a gathering of sorts, you're invited, and immediately your stomach sinks, if you say YES, you'd have to cancel the weekend of *you*. By going to this gathering, whether it be a party, envelope opening, or a cat's funeral, you are going to have to forgo at least half of the things you had planned. You don't really want to go, but there's a lingering *what if* floating above your head. If you do go, things for you will go a little pear shaped, you know this. You will end up doing the groceries late Monday night after work, possibly going hungry all day, starting the week off stressed and behind. For what? A fear of missing out on something. On what exactly? You may not even enjoy the company of a few of the people who are attending but you feel obligated, and you'd hate for people to think badly of you for not going, right? So, you should probably drown out that little voice that is begging for some you time and go, right?

NO. NO. NO. NO. NO.

NO!

By saying yes to an event, out of FOMO and obligation rather than your heart's desire and love, means saying no to you. It means that your desires, your self-worth and your plans aren't important. You're saying that your life, as it is right now, isn't enough, and that is flipping the bird to the universe in a big way. It's not just accepting an invitation. It's RSVP'ing unavailable to your soul's desires. You can't let your soul down. Broken souls aren't fun. SAY, YES TO YOU.

This is something that gets easier with practice. The more you realize that people aren't talking about you— they aren't actually judging your every move—they are usually far too focused on their own lives, then you completely understand your need for self-care. You will begin to honor your intuition more and celebrate what it is that you really need. You know what though, if there are a few people who do decide to weigh in on how exactly it is that you spend your time then there's a Dr. Seuss quote that fits perfectly: "*People that mind don't matter, and people that matter, don't mind.*"

That is all.

FEAR OF BEING STILL

- You work over it.
- You exercise over it.
- You eat over it.
- You clean, bake and sew over it.
- You garden over it.
- You paint over it.
- You socialize, drink and party over it.

Why is it that so many of us have a fear of being still?

I'll take a pretty good guess, it's a fear of our thoughts. It's a fear of what's there and what we may have to face if we hit the pause button on our life and stop running.

STOP RUNNING!

I had to deal with this one as I launched into motherhood with the grace of a heard of hippos. I was working around sixty-five hours a week, until I was thirty-eight weeks pregnant with my son. On the week I finished work, I moved back into our newly renovated home, and I quite literally was go-go-go right up until the birth, where after thirty-three hours and an emergency caesarean, I officially had to surrender.

I was not born knowing how to be his mom. As many new moms know, there is a lot of sitting around loving and nourishing your beautiful new baby. There is *a lot* of late night feeds and quiet time, and while I loved this peanut with all my heart, I was petrified of doing the wrong thing.

All my shit came up. Everything that I had been avoiding over the years bubbled to the surface for me to deal with. Every hiccup, every wrong choice that I had numbed out, pushed down, danced around, exercised over, worked over and run from came up, and it was a mess. I had to deal with each issue one by one. I had to love the wounds. I had to really get to know myself again, all while getting to know my beautiful baby. I really learnt how to calm my farm and slow my roll. I couldn't run anymore. All my old coping mechanisms were taken away from me and I was forced to sit. Forced to heal and it was the best thing I could have done.

What we resist, persists.

I was done running.

You know what though? No two things can exist in the same place at the same time. While letting go of all of my stuff and moving through the hurt, my heart and my soul found space. I created space within myself for something better. I had more room to love and I could choose to live happier and freely.

How did I do this? I got out of my head and back into my body. For every anguished thought or feeling that came up, I followed it. I sat still with it and I asked myself some questions: *Where are you feeling this in your body? What is the issue here? Why does this bother you so much? What have you learnt from this? Can you forgive yourself and them, and move forward?*

And, it always ends with a massive love bomb from me to myself.

Was this always perfect? Hell no. Some thoughts and fears were as persistent as your least favorite song that's stuck on repeat. In some cases, I had to go through these numerous times, and writing letters of release that were never sent often helped, as well as the "write until it's right" action. It takes commitment to the cause, but it was worth it. Some thoughts and fears are pegged so far in the future, that a faithful mindfulness practice which invites you to stay present helps also. Some feelings really suck, some things we move through are heavy, but nothing bites the big one more than being at war with yourself or living in fear. If a thought or feeling persisted after I had consciously done the work, I actively committed to choosing again.

It's time to stop running and stop judging and see what is really there.

By learning the power of my thoughts, I changed the game. I changed the tape. I learnt to love myself again. I'm not talking about the fluffy, pink and poodle-y self-love of the 90s. I am talking about real, raw "I've got your back, you fiery woman" sort of love.

The wearing my heart on the sleeve of a faux leather bomber jacket sort of love. She is love. A real messy, no shame in my game sort of love. A SO WHAT sort of love. A don't f*ck with me sort of love. My loved-up self swears a lot, she's funky and she's fierce and her hair is never neat. She makes bold and vivacious statements, she loves with reckless abandon and her favorite color is WILD. She makes no apologies for loving her coffee, yet she sensibly only has two cups a day. My loved-up self brings the sass but she also loves alone time, daisies and reading nooks. She loves elastic pants and bra free days. She loves family time and meditation. She loves green smoothies and fresh air. She loves sunshine and cold winter nights and that makes perfect sense. She loves connecting with huge crowds and craves quiet time with her thoughts. She is a walking contradiction, but she is OK with that because labels suck and this is her love. Her life. Her story. I learnt to choose again. I am learning to love it *all*. I learnt to love myself. I learnt to be OK with the quiet. I learnt to no longer fear the silence. I learnt to no longer need to fill it.

All of this came from being still. All of this came from getting to know myself.

**When I was busy, I was just fearful.
When I was still,
I became everything else.**

FEAR OF REPEATING THE PAST

Shame is a big one. Regret is huge, and worrying and obsessing over choices in the past can be debilitating. How can we move forward if we keep reading chapters long gone?

I decided many, many years ago now, that I wanted to change my life. That the life I was living didn't feel right within my soul, and some of the situations I found myself in didn't make me feel good about myself. To this day, I don't like to think of them, but I've been making peace with the fact that I'm not perfect, and I will continue to do so for the rest of my days. The only person who was ever harmed in the making of Katie Dean, was Katie Dean, but that still doesn't make the ways I have let myself down in the past any easier to bear. We can be our harshest critics.

Why do we feel that we need to move through life flawlessly? The bumps and twists and the places where we find we have gone the wrong way are the places we get the most growth from. Within our wrong turns are where the lessons are. The places where we develop our character from often break us wide open. They need to because that's where the light gets in. If we never made an error in judgment, we wouldn't be able to speak with such conviction as to what is right for us. Isn't losing your balance and finding out what's important to you all part of the transition from confused and unsure youth to slightly less confused and more open and present adult? If we never made our so-called mistakes, how would we ever grow? Mistakes give us lessons, and lessons make us wiser, and isn't that the point, after all? To become wiser and move through life with a better understanding of who we are, as people, and as hearts walking this Earth. What if we chose to see our wrong turns, as the right ones to this path, and this moment you are in right now. Instead of avoiding and regretting, we appreciate the BLESSON we have been given. Blessing and lesson rolled into one; see what I did there?

This one comes up for me at the oddest of times. You know what though? WHO. CARES. Who cares if you need to face an *oops* you made somewhere on your path. YOU'RE HUMAN. We need to release this expectation that we have always needed to be good in order to be GREAT.

The "good girl" image must die. It's time to let her go, let her move on and say, "sayonara" to her ridiculous expectations.

The way I look at it is if someone is going to judge you for the times when you were feeling the lowest and at your most vulnerable, then they sure as hell don't deserve to be around you at your best.

END SCENE.

Cue the curtain.

NEXT LEVEL IT

As we've just uncovered together, Fear can show up in many, many different forms, and I've got to say I admire her for that. Now, it's time for you to see where she may be hiding or masquerading as something else in your life.

Where do you believe you have been calling FEAR by another name?

What are you planning to do about it?

Not having
walked
a perfectly
straight line
should never
be the
precipice
for staying still.

6

What's Hiding Under Your Bed?

"Roll up! Roll up! All aboard the hot mess express, next stop the shady corners of your psyche."

If you were to actually step aboard this train you would totally see everyone you know. We all have worries, guilt and shame. We all have fears. We all have self-imposed roadblocks.

I shit you not.

We all have our own demons; it's just not everyone is willing to talk about them. It's my mission in life to bring some normalcy to our closeted crazy, because there is such epic and unlimited power in realizing you are not alone.

Side note: Just in case you were wondering and missed that bit ... sweet pea, you are not alone.

Now, I am going to say something that is going to make you feel totally supported and set you free, or I will trigger something in you, either way, get ready.

**Your fears are not special.
What's holding you back
is not unique.**

Gaaaaasp!

Your fears are not more valid, more important, or scarier than anyone else's. The only difference is that they are stopping *you*, and not *them*. Your fears are however special to you. They have somehow ruffled your feathers in a big way and I have no doubt that to you they may be bat shit scary. I know you believe this to be true, and in this moment, before you take one step further, I'm going to let you have that.

Your fears are a VERY big deal.

See how much better that feels. I'm not ever going to try and talk you out of your fears. I'm not ever going to try and sugar coat your scaries, or gloss over what worries you because that shit you are feeling is real. On this note, I should say, when one of your favorite people in the world comes to you with an issue and they are all caught up in what's flustering them, just listen. Hold the space. Hold her tight. Be there. Don't explain or brush her fears away because in that moment, the best thing she can do is move through them.

When your best friend has lost this battle, and is face-to-face with her own internal war.

When your sister loses out on a dream come true, or the man she loves leaves.

When her expectations are shattered, please don't spout on how expectations are bad. She hoped, she lost.

Give her THIS.

One of the worst things you can say to someone who is hurting is, "everything happens for a reason." In that moment, the only thing she can feel or see is the heaviness of her heart and the weight of the disappointment. Disappointment or despair doesn't discriminate, and when expectations are dashed, it bites the big one. There is a time and a place for pep talks and motivation, but it's not when she's hurting, it's not after the initial blow, it's not when she feels broken.

Let her have THAT.

Don't discount her pain. Don't try and gloss over her anguish with shitty cliché bumper sticker phrases. Let her feel what she needs to feel and move through the emotions. Don't attempt to dam up the river. Don't attempt to stop the tears, they are there to cleanse the soul, we all need a good cry every now and then. The storm cleanses us.

It's not easy to watch your loved one hurt.

It's not easy to know what to say when shit hits the fan and all you want to do is help.

It's not easy to know what to do when your face-to-face with someone else's suffering. It's scary. You feel helpless. You panic.

Instead ... let her have THIS.

Hold the Space.

Hold the space for as long as she needs, for as many conversations as it takes, until the tears run dry.

Be brave in the face of her sadness, of her confusion, of her rage even.

Understanding the situation comes in time, but now is not the time to be reminding someone of this. There will be a time and place to get the pom-poms out, but let her show you when that is. Advice is best accepted when asked for.

Sometimes the best way you can show your love and support is to not try and change the situation, but to stand alongside her and support her.

She chose you. She loves you. She's your friend, sister, daughter, colleague.

Give her THIS.

If we can alter the way we stand alongside our fear and in turn, someone else's, the world will always get a little braver.

Now, in this chapter, we are going to turn the lights on.

Your fear and your ego love to live in the deepest darkest corners of your mind. Your fear is a bit of a loner, a bit of a lurker, kind of an outcast, but we are going to change that.

Somewhere along the line in this beautiful ride called life, something has happened to help you form an opinion, or helped you to formulate a reaction to something. We aren't born fearing things, we are a product of our environment and every single experience that we have had up until now. These fears and these stories are all part of the equation. They are just something we have decided to carry as our truth.

We are born fearless, full of marvel and wonder. We are explorers and risk takers, and full of inspiration and mystery, and I have witnessed this first hand, through the eyes of my son. The world is a wild and exciting place and he is constantly looking to me, to gauge my reactions to everything he does to see what's safe, what's scary and what he should be worried about. My fears become his fears, so I am really conscious of not projecting my concerns on to him.

I spend my days endeavoring to keep him safe, but curious. Watching him and guiding him has confirmed something for me—**we learn fear**.

We learn our thoughts. We have been conditioned to look at things a certain way, and just as you have learnt it, you can unlearn.

True Story

You can create new neural pathways. You can choose to see things a different way, and yes, it's going to take commitment from you, but you know what, living small takes a shit load of energy too.

I was first introduced to the concept of "re-wiring" our "hard wiring" aka, neural pathways when I was on my very first and let's be honest, only, *Gwinganna Lifestyle Retreat.*

Every day we had the option to attend lectures on a vast range of topics from the benefits of raw foods, to toilet poo habits, to the way our mind works and how we can actually teach ourselves to think a different way. In fact, it's stuck with me so much so that it was another one of those lightbulb moments where everything became possible.

It can take as little as six weeks to totally change your thought process, and re-program your belief system to evoke and follow a new way to be.

Six weeks! That's nothing.

I was running fitness programs that were twice as long as that four times a year. So, for me, the possibility that could be created through the power of positive thinking when partnered with commitment to healthy lifestyle choices that reflect your desired life, when partnered with a consistent attempt at calling in the feelings you wish to embody, the sky became the limit. What had once felt like a dark cloud now became the thing that would allow me to practice on myself, so I could then help others do the same. You can't teach something that you don't completely understand yourself. This is now a craft I practice daily, and I can say with one hundred percent certainty that I have now changed my default settings.

My go-to when things go wrong or get tricky is no longer pity or despair. I have taught myself to look for the possibility in chaos. Just like it's possible to teach yourself to brush your teeth with the opposite hand. You can teach yourself a brand new normal with a whole new outlook.

You can totally do this, it's simply one decision at a time.

A commitment to choosing the light, an awareness of what's going on with your emotions and the willingness to choose again, even if it feels like you're moving a mountain to do so.

It's always and only ever about choosing the next right thing.

Through periods of writing this book, I am often greeted by a familiar friend. At times, I find myself working through some challenging emotional stuff as my mind, even with all its understanding of what it's up to, likes to pull a few swift ones. There's been many a curve ball within these words, so believe me when I tell you, my catching arm is SHARP.

I will never be free of my active mind and these day's I'm choosing to see it as a gift. I am a sensitive soul by nature. I'm a passionate feely person but I can thrive with it. I can understand it. I can always move through it and the divine timing isn't lost on me.

At this point, in sharing my words, I'm having trouble sleeping. Every night, I am turning my fear into bravery. Every time I feel that adrenaline surge as my beautifully active mind wants to attach to something and react, I am using the tools within this book, embracing my signals and changing the game. Sometimes, I nail it and feel ten-feet-tall, sometimes I miss the mark, but with each new sunrise I reset.

Living a fearful life is not for me, I'm just not that keen on it to be honest, but come on now, WHO IS? It takes far more energy to stay scared than what it does to commit to a life well-loved and lived. It makes far more sense to be putting that focus, that energy into something that you do want, and into creating, rather than running from something.

The thing is, I now know these anxious times will always pass.

And so, it did.

Next Level It

We are creatures of habit and we love patterns. We habitually relive the same situation over and over and we will continue to do so until it teaches us what we need to learn.

I know, you know, the areas of your life that come with that all too familiar feeling you'd rather live without, and I know that the mixed tape that plays around those times can start to wear you down, so let's change it.

What is the internal dialogue in your default settings that plays before you unravel?

How does that feel within your body?

After you acknowledge its presence. What can you change it too?

How does that feel within your body? Call it in, feel the way you want to feel and choose to embody a thought and feeling that empowers you, not drowns you.

That-a-girl.
Lather. Rinse.
Rrepeat.
It's always and
only ever
about choosing
the next
right thing.

7

MOVING THROUGH

N ow, that I've gone all Adele, on this latest phase and can now say, "Hello from the other side." I see how the cycle of freak out kept me in this fearful place, and do you want to know the biggest load of horse shit that came out of it?

The fearful thought that, I am destined to feel this way forever.

What a damaging lie that was, yet for a moment, my beautiful creative mind accepted that this was it. That I was forever meant to live in fear and that I may as well just get on with it.

F-THAT!

F- THAT in a big way.

F- THAT thought to hell because that's where it came from.

I am a Queen.

I am the commander of this ship and this is NOT how my story is going to end.

Thank goodness.

EVERYTHING CHANGED.

One of the most powerful and comforting things a person can hear when they are going through something is, "Me too." There's something that shifts when you are going through a heavy time emotionally when you hear about someone else's shitty time and they can mirror that back for you. It's even better when they have lived it, learnt from it and continued to go on loving with it as part of their past and thriving alongside their shadows.

Someone who is very dear to me, is Amy Mackenzie from *Designing Her Life*. She is one of the most generous, capable and warm souls, I have ever met. Her eyes glow, she wears her heart on her sleeve and she talks with such beautiful conviction.

Amy's story surprised me when I heard it. Not because it's uncommon, because we do hear about it often, but because of the woman she is because of it.

Amy had a really hard upbringing. She was raised a Jehovah's Witness, with the sort of financial struggles you read about. Amy has spoken to me about situations where she had to steal toilet paper from public bathrooms for her and her family to have such a basic necessity.

Amy left home at a young age on a mission to leave her upbringing behind her; she was more determined than ever not to allow her story to dictate her future. This woman worked several jobs, saved as much as she could, and at the age of nineteen, could finally afford to get her license, only to be part of a car accident that would change the trajectory of her life forever.

While this accident wasn't horrific in stature, the

ramifications for Amy were life changing. Through the impact, it was as though a switch was flicked in Amy's brain and she now lives with a condition known as Chronic Pain Syndrome. It took three years of debilitating symptoms, hundreds of doctors and specialists visits, and cocktails of drugs to attempt to manage the pain, with no success, to be given this diagnosis.

Any day, all day, Amy is in some degree of pain. For a few years, it was crippling and her inspiring go get 'em attitude for life faded away. If you knew the "live your life to the fullest" type girl I know today, I knew I had to get her to share her insights from one of life's harshest challenges, so far. Amy's thoughts changed from a belief in her ability to achieve anything to things like: *This isn't fair, life was already really hard. I did my best, I worked my ass off to get beyond that and now this has happened? Why? Maybe I'm not meant for more.*

From there things got even worse and Depression and Anxiety set in.

It was at this point, Amy gave up on hope, her life and her struggle, and awoke to find herself in a Hospital bed having survived.

From there, things were different. In that bed, in what many would describe as her darkest hour, Amy chose to find the light and since has been determined to make every day better than the last.

Amy shares: I stopped blaming, I stopped thinking of everything that had happened to me and how unfair it was and I started to look at what I could do. What power did I have over the life that I had now? I said goodbye to the life that I had kept dreaming of, that I kept thinking I should be living, and wasn't, and I made peace with the fact that this was my life now. How could I make the best of this life? That was huge, that started to really change things.

The biggest thing for me was taking accountability. Obviously, there are things that happen to us that we don't ask for, we don't want, and we wouldn't wish upon anyone. It's not about trying to shift the blame to other people or things, even though, it may be someone else's fault what has happened, or it may be an unfair circumstance or card that you get dealt. When I talk about the accountability side it's because we can take back our power in how we react to it, how we respond and what we do with it. For me, the biggest moment was when I knew to stop looking at all the things that could have or should have happened, or being upset that these things have happened to me. Instead, I started to ask, where can I take back my power? And, I got there through taking accountability for the things that I could control.

Gratitude was also a huge factor in Amy's recovery and is still a huge part of her message to the world. Amy is now an international speaker, an amazing life coach for entrepreneurs, has a thriving business, is a big dreamer and someone I call a dear friend.

Amy's story is one of many brave women I know that teaches us; it can't always be peace, love and mung beans. Everything is always moving and evolving and there are *always* options when you realize that you get to decide what the next page of your story will be. There is a way through every block if you are ready to *dare greatly*, be vulnerable and have the conversations that matter.

We can't have the light without darkness, in fact, the moon has a partnership with the sun. They both have a place, they both occupy the same space and while the moon makes waves, the sun warms the soul, and so it is.

I love that I am sensitive, I love that I feel things so deeply and I love that I am understanding myself, my makeup, more and more each day. I now know that

you can't truly love yourself, until you get to know yourself and are open to staying in touch with who that is as you grow.

I will always have a monkey mind, but for now the zoo is resting and I will not feed the fears. All our emotions are valid. All our feelings have purpose, but when the night is at its darkest, it's hard to imagine that it could ever make way for then sun ... but it does.

**The only way to navigate
these anxious and tumultuous times
we find ourselves in,
is to stay true and move through.
Nothing lasts forever.**

You are a beautiful resilient masterpiece and if you are down in the trenches now, keep going. The sun will show its face again soon and the waves of the moon will make way for your calm and sparkling sea.

I urge you, if you are feeling blue or low, to reach out, talk to your tribe, your healers, your friends and do whatever it takes to help you move through. Exhaust every option, commit to honoring what you need, and do whatever it takes to stand tall and strong again.

You Don't Have to Believe Everything You Think!

If your beautiful mind is trying to convince you that things will never change or get better, you just tell it, "you ain't seen nothin' yet" and, paint your life with all the colors of the rainbow.

Decide today that you are not your thoughts but the gal who gets to hear them. Start to choose the ones you take on as your truth. Commit to this and one day soon, you will be handing out sunglasses because the sun has come around again and it's just so darn bright.

Never be afraid to call BULLSHIT on your thoughts, sometimes you have to call your own bluff.

In this world, when you can get almost anything RIGHT NOW, the idea that lifelong happiness takes lifelong commitment has many running for the hills when it comes to living with anxiety and fear.

I will never stop searching. I will never stop loving and I will never stop supporting myself as I learn to ride the waves that come my way.

COWA-FREAKEN-BUNGA DUDE, surf is up!

I am a big believer in moving forward and not looking back, but for the purpose of finding the seed that planted the tree that is shading your dreams, go with me.

Have you ever stopped to think where your insecurities come from? Where is the moment in your life's story that you decided: *YEP, I'm not ever going to get on stage because I'm not good enough*, or *I couldn't possibly work in that career because I need to be more outspoken than I am*, or *I could never write, paint, sculpt, create because I don't have the time or the talent.*

These are all real thoughts, but I guarantee none of these are true.

You can do absolutely anything in this world. You can.

The possibilities are limitless. You have the power to step up and step out and do whatever it is that you enjoy. What you don't have control of is the outcome.

No one does.

We are free in this world to make anything, do anything, live any way we like, but we can't control the outcomes.

So how do you get past that? You let go of your attachment to the result and you do the thing because it makes you happy not because of what it will afford you.

It's rarely ever the event, the task, the THING that scares you, it's the outcome that follows suit which holds you back.

Lose your attachment to outcomes and find joy within the process.

BOO-YAH!

NEXT LEVEL IT

I am offering you front row seats to the best show in town, your mind.

If you're willing, it's time to start paying attention to the narration you're giving your life's movie.

Become a witness to your thoughts.

Without judgment and without expectations start paying attention to the way you are communicating with yourself and see exactly what the *Story* is that you're telling yourself about the situations within your life.

What to do with the information you uncover? That's entirely up to you.

Remember though, you *can* choose again. You *can* change the way you look at things as many times as you like. Anything that doesn't support the way you wish to view yourself and the world you live in can be changed, and you, my friend, have the power to create a world that supports you in every way.

Stay true
and
move through.

8

WHEN FEAR ATTACKS

L et's get clear on something. To think that, I, who was called to write a book on bravery, would have no fears, or go through life without experiencing anxiety, or dread or just a general sense of foreboding at times would be flat out wrong.

I get scared. I get really scared, but more often than not, I get my miracle and I can move through it with ease, and other times like last night, I end up down a rabbit hole. This particular time, I was so far over my head I couldn't find my way out.

My husband was away for the weekend at his niece's wedding, and Archer and I couldn't go because my little man doesn't travel so well. Seven hours in the car just didn't seem like a fair option.

After a few big days of adulating and mom-ing, I was all set for a quiet night in watching *Gilmore Girls* on DVD, fake shopping online and indulging in a chocolate muggin' for dessert. I was also scrolling through Facebook when everything went pear shaped. I saw something, my mind turned to work and it triggered me. My anxiety hit fever pitch and I started to spiral.

All the *what ifs* started circling.

I started second guessing myself. I started thinking about all the work I had to do, if I had finished things up properly, answered all my emails, or if I was doing enough. I started worrying about the future and making plans for my newsletter and blog, and what wouldn't normally cause me to bat an eyelid, somehow did. The day's events and the mood I was in left a window open for a spiral of freak out and because I wasn't expecting it, I hit panic stations.

Mindfulness helped, but I was still a little edgy. My anxiety was on red alert and ready to attach to anything and everything. Of course, right before bed another thought popped in, my fear travelled down another tangent, and POW.

This one got me.

I couldn't talk my way around this super fun little episode and after meditating, reading, a million trips to the bathroom for nervous wees, a small time sitting under the stars, more reading and I think I even tried cleaning my teeth, I knew, I just had to ride it out, weather the storm and that's OK too.

The energy just needed to move through me, the adrenaline just had to be reabsorbed and from this wild ride, I learnt to appreciate the magnificence of the power of my thoughts and the chemical responses that occur within my body when in fear. They are pretty F-ing remarkable.

Once the second hit of adrenalin from my worry bomb entered my system I just had to allow my body, and my mind to move through it.

I surrendered.

Today, as I write this, the morning after, I have an anxiety hangover and it's rough. Today, I am committed to a day of no pressure. A day of forgiveness and a day where I am not striving to have a totally uplifting, super positive and constructive day. Today is just going to be what it is.

Today I am just going to have a *day*.

Of course, now that I have given myself the space to do whatever I feel like and just relax and play with Archer, I have created room for the answers to flow through me and there's some nuggets of gold in them there hills, friends.

Fear and worry are powerful motivators and I respect them.

I have a mind that can deduct every possible outcome in .2 seconds and that needs to be OK with me. This just means I will have a life where I am always given the option to choose love over fear in its simplest and most beautiful form, and each time I am able to do that, it's a miracle.

Now, I accept a life with anxiety as one of my back up dancers, but sometimes, I like to ask why she feels the need to hustle up to front row center. #showpony

There is always a lesson in every dalliance with fear, we just need to ask the right questions. So, when the time was right and the baby was asleep I got a little real with myself and it was time for some beautiful self-enquiry.

My trigger: What was the underlying vibe of why I felt so scared?

The blessing: Where is the lesson in this?

What came up for me was this ... **I am enough**.

No task, no schedule, no launch is as important as the way I view myself and the message I share at the table.

My truth: I have to let what I do in my work be enough.

I have to trust that what I share is of benefit to others, as well as myself, and that I always check-in with what I need and what moves me and honor that.

I choose the path.
I create the rules.

I define success on my terms because this is a beautiful passion that needs to fit in with my life, not the other way around.

My message is my truth, my truth is my happiness and my happiness brings my magic. I do what I do because I love it and I need to be sure to love what I do. I create what I create because I love to share my experiences. I share what I share because I've been there, I'm walking it. There's solidarity in the sisterhood. I teach what I teach because it has worked for me, and if it works for you, then HELL YEAH TO THAT!

I can't control people's perceptions of me. I can only control the way I show up and if I show up with the best intention, then that has to be enough.

I Am Enough

However, that looks is perfect.

Second thing that surfaced ... **Guilt is a useless emotion**.

As a mom, there are always going to be things we feel we can do better. As a mom, I will always worry if I have done what's best for my son and that is all part of the parcel. I will always want to check on him one last time, before bed. I will always want to hug him a little longer and I will always do anything to see him smile.

What I do know for sure is that guilt is a waste of energy, it doesn't serve any other purpose other than to keep us future trippin', living in the past, or frolicking in regret. I have no intention of fostering a place for this energy to fester. All I can do is my best. All I can do is keep Archer as safe and as happy as I have the ability to, and the rest is out of my hands. I know I'm not perfect and I am figuring it out as I go. I have given myself permission to love fiercely and still make mistakes and carry on for always. I have also given myself permission to find motherhood a really tough gig and still love my son with the passion of a thousand suns. One doesn't cancel the other out.

Some realizations aren't fun, sometimes you have to step back and admit you are being ridiculous. Once we realize and become aware of our thoughts and our fears we can work on accepting them, healing them and moving past them.

Every time I see these thoughts, witness the triggers and feel myself spiraling around these issues, I can spring into action like a super tropical gazelle. I can choose to support myself, encourage myself and nurture myself.

BEAUTIFUL CHALLENGE ACCEPTED

I will try not to judge, but I will most certainly FORGIVE. Forgiveness is the cornerstone to so many of our beautiful growth opportunities. Today, I chose to forgive myself for listening to my busy mind and losing site of my **why**.

I forgive myself for trying to predict and micromanage my life and for doubting my ability. I accept what my best is and I release the need to control my life. The universe has my back.

NOTHIN. BUT. NET.

NEXT LEVEL IT

How do you process your fear?

Prevention, of course, is better than any cure, but I don't ever want us to strive for a world without fear. I want us instead to be strong enough within ourselves that we embrace our fears and learn to be one with the fire.

In preparation for our moments, all aglow, I want you to be clear on a little Soulful Action Plan. There's a reason we have fire drills and safety demonstrations; think of this as a resuscitation plan for your soul.

How do you plan to handle your fear and your worries moving forward when they show up for you?

What tools will you use from your spiritual toolkit?

How will you choose to perceive your fear from this day forward?

It feels so much better to have that sorted out, doesn't it?

I choose
the path.
I create
the rules.

9

It's Not Always as It Seems

Not every act of bravery is marked by an external step forward. Some of the biggest and most profound actions of badassery come from the moments where time stands still and we venture within.

You cannot keep serving yourself up the same poo-pie for breakfast an expect it to taste different. You can't honestly expect a different outcome if the method in making your meal is the same. If you are living the same lesson over and over again, you need to turn the page, try a new menu or find out what ingredient is *eff-ing* up your masterpiece.

Let's workshop this again.

Cause vs effect: Take a look at what ruffles you.

Is it the event and situation that scares you, or the fact that you can't control the outcome and fear the uncontrollable instead?

For instance, with my panic-party just gone. Of course, I wasn't really worried about the emails, they can wait, but I was worried that I would have missed something important and people would think I'm incompetent for not responding sooner. I was really worried about being judged.

Or say, you wanted to change careers. It's probably not the prospect of starting a new job that's the issue, it's the: *What if I fail? What if I'm not good enough for this role? What if I make a fool of myself?*

And people saying, "I told you so."

- **Fear of the outcome.**
- **Fear of the Outcome.**
- **Fear. Of. The. Outcome.**

That is all, even though, we have already established that we can't predict the future, right? So, really you are worrying about nothing, CORRECT?

Are you really going to let a whole bunch of *what ifs* stand in the way of you and your dreams of living a life filled with experiences and color?

I didn't think so. So, now what?

> **What if you saw these challenges,**
> **circumstances and experiences**
> **as nothing more than**
> **a chance to be brave?**

What if you saw them as a chance to live?

- **To grow.**
- **To learn more about yourself.**
- **To understand yourself.**
- **To expand.**

YOUR FEAR IS A CHANCE FOR YOU TO BE BRAVE.

What if, you did the thing purely for the sheer enjoyment and exhilaration it provides you with rather than white knuckling it and trying to control the outcome?

What if you sat down with this uncomfortable vibe and had a little heart to heart and said, "Hey, Miss Fear, I know you are getting all up in my face about THIS, but what's the real vibe to your jibe?"

Could it be that you are actually trying to hide the fact that you don't like—fill in the appropriate truth bomb here—about yourself? Or perhaps, you're placing too much of your happiness in the opinions of others. This is a choice you can make and a conversation you can have. You can choose to use that bat signal, which is really those physical changes within your body as a chance to rise up. It no longer has to mean what it used to. That signal can become a beacon for courage, inquiry, personal growth, bravery, authenticity, while they may seem like the same thing, they are all beautifully different.

Today, you can choose to flip the switch, change the program and create a new relationship with your emotions.

You decide what they mean.

You can delve a little deeper.

You decide who leads the charge and you decide what's worth it and what's not.

It's all up to you, you can ask the questions, you can delve a little deeper, and you *can* choose again.

This brings me to a theory I like to use, and believe me, I use if OFTEN.

It's my "F- it" theory.

I am a massive advocate of being a spiritually savvy woman. We don't need saving, we have this shit handled, but we need to come correct. We need to be packing the goods, and those goods come in the form of a spiritual tool box. This toolbox is filled with all the tools and tricks and life hacks you have collected on this wild ride.

Every situation, every fear, every hurdle, or prickly patch we have to navigate, requires a different set of tools. It's kind of like hanging a picture. Every wall and picture combo will require you to use something different. For example, a simple gyprock wall in your home might require a hammer and nail. If you come across an almighty mother-of-a-brick-wall, you'll be needing yourself a drill and a screw. Because you've gathered the tools along the way, you have the goods available to you when needed and you can find a way through every decorating emergency.

Same thing applies to life.

As you shimmy, slide, and stumble your way through life you acquire more knowledge, more skills and a far better understanding of what you will need to find a way through every block. There are times though, when there is only one solution, and I use this simple yet effective tool daily.

If you have shone a light on your fears, said your affirmations, chosen again, turned it around, shared it with a friend, learnt a lesson, had a chat to it, found a four-leaf clover, held an abundance circle, stood on your head and hugged a unicorn and you are still not feeling it. I want you to take a deep breath, stand tall, look your fear straight in the eye and say, "FUCK IT." Then do it anyway.

Sometimes there are no other words.

I use this theory daily. I pull it out over big life changing decisions, over what to have for breakfast. Over whether or not to go to the bathroom before I go for a run or wait until I get home. It helps me when I'm anxious and over my own bullshit. It's my spiritual dose of Red Bull. It gives me wings before a life changing event or a simple nervous phone call.

The F-IT theory never lets me down. It's a cheeky, throw caution to the wind—kind of, don't mess with me—world sass packed statement. Use it to your hearts content and I bet you feel it's power.

NEXT LEVEL IT

You are going to invite the duffle bag toting, socially awkward, previously outcast friend to the table and you are going to get to know her a little better, "Come on over Fear, feel free to take a seat."

The best way to take the scary out of the darkest parts of your story, is to shine a light on everything that keeps you living in the shadows. The way that this works best is to take these thoughts from your mind and put them on paper. The reason a brain dump like this works so well is because suddenly, your worries become crystal clear. You can't argue with a piece of paper and I've never *not* been shocked at how much smaller my fears and concerns are on paper than what they were in my mind.

If you have ever made a list in your mind to go to the grocery store it always feels as though it's a mile long.

This is because your brain keeps having the same thoughts, with tiny tweaks just to keep it fresh.

It might sound something like: *Oh, my goodness, I have to get a bunch of things from the shop, I don't know how I'm going to get all of this done quickly. I need bread, milk, tomatoes, almonds and dog food. I better not forget anything. I need milk, bread, dog food, almonds and tomatoes. Will, I need a trolley, or can I use a basket? I need dog food, bread, tomatoes, milk and almonds ... oh, God, I don't want to forget anything, bread, tomatoes...*

The list feels huge, your day feels heavier than what it actually is and the reality is usually far from that. The second you write the list down, you see it's only four things and incredibly doable.

Free writing is such a beautiful and powerful tool and there is no right way to do it. Do it just the way that feels right for you. It's not about judgment, it doesn't even have to make sense. It's just about letting it all flow freely.

Taking it from the swirling fear bomb that resides in your melon to the blank canvas that is a piece of paper is the goal; how that looks, is *how* it looks.

I've had quite a few clients afraid to take on this task for fear of what will come up, or a fear that they will never be able to finish writing once they start. I can totally relate. I have had some totally *awks* moments during this exercise myself where it becomes so paramount that I need to sit through some heavy and uncomfortable emotions and memories. The thing is though, it's better out than in, and if you're going on a bear hunt, you can't go over it, you can't go under it, you have to go through it.

If you want to feel lighter, live brighter and be free of your hurt or fears then you first have to acknowledge that they exist. If you keep pushing them down then you will never truly be free of them and you will forever in some way, shape or form, *be stuck.*

All great things are preceded by chaos and if you're avoiding this exercise, it's time to ask yourself why. The discomfort can't hurt you. These thoughts are just thoughts and it is time you set yourself free.

When you're ready, here are some prompts to guide you into free writing the shizzle out of your story.

What am I most afraid of?

Be sure to get real here ... look below the surface.

- **Why am I letting it hold me back?**
- **What can I learn from this?**
- **What can I do to move through this?**

When you have brought your fears out into the real world on paper in all its glory, you can you see them for what they are. Can you see that they are just a story that you have attached to a situation? Your thoughts are totally powerless until you give them power. Today, in this moment, it's time to take your power back.

Make a
different
meal
or you'll get
the same
brearfast.

10

WHEN POSITIVE THINKING GOES BAD

So, there I was, sixteen-weeks pregnant with our beautiful IVF baby, our second child, sitting on my bed absolutely seething.

Furious that I was feeling this same way *yet* again. This is where I would usually calm my farm, think positive thoughts, try and see things another way, and commit to finding a different way to approach things tomorrow.

Not this time.

This time, on this evening, in this instance, something came over me and for the first time, I actually saw things *as* they were. It was a moment of pure clarity, synergy and energy—a dedication to my love of life came over me, and next thing you know—I was throwing back the covers, taking my pudgy pregnant self to announce to my then husband that, "I CAN'T!" I had no intention of asking for a separation but that is where it ended because all signs were pointing me to YES.

I truly had no other words for the most part and my soul had spoken up for me because I physically, emotionally and spiritually could no longer.

"I can't!"

In the moments and days that followed and all the questions from others around me, when left trying to explain exactly why I had made the final call, all the reasons *why* were there and completely understandable: two simple words summed up what years and years of situations had me feeling, "I CAN'T!"

When you ask for signs from the universe, you better be ready to see what is presented. When the universe steps in (ahem … it's always on your side), you are inevitably opening up a Pandora's box because once things are seen, they can't be unseen, and I was given all the signs and signals I needed. Even though, this was spoken about many times between us, gauntlets thrown down and lines drawn in the sand, I had always remained *in* my marriage. Always willing to try again, to forgive, to attempt to understand, to believe in another … Always.

Until I wasn't.

In that moment, a power and clarity that wasn't my own came over me and forced me to listen.

I will never forget that night, it was both the bravest and scariest thing I've ever done, and I truly had no idea when I woke up that morning, that this was the day that would forever divide my life. This was now going to divide everything into my before and after.

In the weeks that followed, I never wavered in my decision, and to this day I know why and I know this is for the best. Hindsight is always 20/20 and one thing that astounds me is the way that I allowed the situation to continue for so long. I did though, through hope, optimism and the power of positive thinking and I realized something pretty profound, sometimes positive thinking can go bad.

"WHAAAAAAT?" I hear you say.

I KNOW, RIGHT?

I realized that I had used the power of positive thinking to sweep over, glance past, sweep under the rug, and some serious things that were actually situations that should have served as signs, and probably should have been felt and dealt with in a different way.

SHIT!

This realization was one of epic proportions, but I refuse to do all the should-a-could-a-would-a on myself. I truly believe that everything happened as it was meant to and if it hadn't played out the way it did, I wouldn't be carrying my beautiful little man in my belly and I wouldn't have the clarity of mind I have today. Part of me believes this extra strength has come from this tiny little babe himself which is truly pretty magical. If it wasn't for him and knowing that he was now feeling everything I was, I may have never taken the action, or the stand that I did, and I still would be enabling, validating and allowing my life to continue as it was.

I've learnt something through this dark time. In fact, I've learnt more than I ever thought, I didn't understand and that alone, is comforting.

We aren't always meant to see with rose colored glasses.

We aren't always meant to see the glass as half full.

We aren't always meant to see if we can see things another way because something's are as simple and as straightforward as they seem. We need to quit giving them the subtext and the back story that makes certain behaviors or situations OK.

END SCENE.

Some *things* that happen in life will hurt us, and some people make decisions, or painful mistakes and it's not our job to sugar coat that for them.

Some actions hurt and if the same situation in life keeps repeating itself, it's not an accident or a mistake, it is, in fact, a choice and what we do with that is then up to us.

I'm not just talking about romantic relationships, I'm talking about any situation where you feel "less than" during or afterwards as a result. This could be the case with work, family, or friendships.

Sure, you can totally find another way to see it and try to see the positive as part of the healing, but first, I now see that it's important for us to *feel* it. To lean in and really let the situation that presents itself marinade, before we seal it with a kiss and sweep it under the totally cool boho rug.

I totally get that it's zero fun to feel some of these totally unwelcome feelings, and we want to get the yuk part over and done with ASAP, but these dark times are really important for us and for our understanding of our NOW.

Emotions are always energy and if you choose to bottle these bad boys up they'll fester and grow and before you know it, you've created your very own emotional volcano and woman, that beauty is going to BURST!

We live in a world where we try and fix everything and we try and fix it fast. We want everything to be smooth sailing and pain free, but if you constantly deny yourself the depths of your emotions, you will spend your life in the shallow end of the pool and let's be honest, that's where all the kids are peeing.

The second I allowed myself to feel, to go deep, to go in, I surrendered.

I stopped seeing things as I believed they could be, and started seeing things as they are, and this was not the end. This was not the conclusion to everything I knew and trusted as I'd feared. This was the beginning of healing and a whole new sort of freedom.

When we create a world, in our own mind and have to work incredibly hard, day in and day out to keep the illusion going—constantly searching for the good, constantly seeking out the lesson, constantly dusting ourselves off—it's really freaken exhausting.

If you are in a role for work or life that is taking that much of your soul to keep it going, you have got to ask yourself, WHY?

Why are you having to work so hard to find the beauty in it?

What are you having to constantly compromise to find your happiness?

Why is your happiness a separate part of the conversation to begin with?

Super important questions friends, and ones that should always be answered the second they arise, instead of being put in the pile that may lead you down a path that you're not ready for.

The thing is though, seeing things for what they really are doesn't have to mean walking away from them. It doesn't have to always mean that it's not meant for you and the fit isn't right. It may just mean that you can officially resign as the creator and CEO of the universe, and start to make your decisions based on what is right in front of you, not what you would like them to be.

You may have an asshole of a boss. That's OK. When you know what you're dealing with. Send them love and light and make decisions based on how you want to proceed.

You may have a shitty relationship with a family member. No *probs*. See it for what it is, feel what you need to feel and decide how much of them you want to allow in your life. You get to choose your circle.

As for relationships, well that's the same sort of thing. If you are white knuckling it trying to hold on and feel the way you think you should, then sure you can keep doing that. I'm certainly not going to point a finger, but if that's not feeling right to you, you can also see what happens when you resign as the "fixer" and see things for what they really are.

You might even find a whole new middle ground and respect for what you have, which is rad, or you may see that what you thought you had was never actually there in the first place. Both of those options are always open to interpretation and both will set you free.

Emotions are nothing but energy in motion. They can't hurt us. They can't keep us stuck. We are the ones who build the dams or block the passage. We are the ones who don't allow them to provide the messages they are meant to and the insights they were sent with. We are the only ones who can change the pattern, open the doors, feel what it is that we need to feel to become the women we were destined to be.

**Give yourself the gift of
the FULL experience.**

Once you have finally allowed yourself to go deep, to feel the feels and see the world as it truly is, THAT is when you get to decide on how you wish to interpret the situation. That is when you get to choose a perspective that supports your view in life and THAT is where you get to seek out the lesson and choose your direction.

Think of it like a bee sting. It's kind of like a 4-step process.

THE IMPACT

You've been bitten.

The incident occurs in your life and it stings, it hurts so bad and you're in shock because hellooo, BEES.

FEAR SETS IN

"Holy shit! This hurts, this really hurts!"

You wonder if you're ever going to feel OK again, you wonder how long this pain will last and you instantly go searching for anything that will make the pain stop. Like RIGHT NOW.

DENIAL

It's OK, it will pass, it's just a little bee sting, right?

If I don't think about it, it will go away. I just have to keep busy with something else.

SURRENDER

You were just stung by a fucking bee!

Give the toxin a chance to do its thing, run its course, then leave your body and all will be well. Then and only then when you've felt all you need to feel can you decide if it's a good idea to work barefoot in the garden next time, and make a more *informed* choice.

If you really think about it, how many times have we rushed for the quick fix in our lives to feel better immediately? If you do that, you are missing the part where you get to see that you survived and made it through all by yourself. You not only survived, but you thrived and gained a far better understanding of how the world works and the views that you hold about your world in it.

If you rush for the **pain away** spray, not only will you miss the healing, you will probably develop a fear of bees, fuel your anxiety and cause yourself long-term psychological pain, for a superficial short-term gain.

DON'T RUSH THE MIDDLE

It's usually the fear of the fall out that has us rushing for our tools to fix everything, but if we skip over the deep emotions before choosing a perspective that supports us, we miss the **gold** that will sustain us an empower us for **life**.

**Give yourself the gift of
resilience and healing.
You are far more capable
than you think.**

I have just gone through, and am going through the thing that I feared most for years, and I am here, I am surviving, and sure some days are "cry on the bathroom floor" hard, but those days were there before and there were a lot of them. As well as those oh-so heavy gray days, a whole heap of anger, and suppressed emotions that I wasn't allowing myself to feel.

That stuff is **H.E.A.V.Y.** and I want to teach my two little ones about strength and resilience, and the strongest thing I could do for them and for me was to lighten the load.

It may sound counter intuitive but it's really where your true strength lies.

- **Release control.**
- **Resign as CEO of the Universe.**
- **Allow it to be what it is.**

END SCENE.

Next Level It

I know that it can feel scary and overwhelming to toy with the notion of opening up the floodgates of what's real and what is there to be felt. There's a fear that the hurting won't stop, or that you will stay stuck in the darkness, but that couldn't be further from the truth.

As I said before, emotions are fluid. They are energy in motion and they are designed to pass through and share their wisdom along the way. If you continually try and sugar coat it, run from it and hide it from others, that's a whole lot of "life tidying" that you're doing in order to prepare for your guests.

You don't live in a museum. Your "home" isn't on display for the world, it's there for you to live in and if you want to put your feet up and leave some crap on the floor to better decide if you want to keep it or not, then let it be so.

Where in your life are you working extra hard at holding on?

What are you afraid to feel?

What is the worst thing that could possibly happen?

And if it does, what would you do?

Then what would you do?

Then what would you do?

Keep doing this until you get to the place where you survived, rocked on and allowed your life to unfold as it could.

I am a huge advocate of the "Then What" game. It has helped one hundred per cent of the time and I know it will for you too.

**You are far more capable
than you give yourself credit for.**

You are a **survivor** and you have survived every single shitty day in your life up until this point, so don't bottle up all the feels now.

Give yourself the full experience and explore the many dimensions of your reality.

It's actually pretty cool.

You can't outrun

Pain

in the pusuit of

Happiness.

11

FINDING YOUR WINGS

When I talk to clients about confidence, the biggest hurdle for them is often the fact that they are worried that they won't be liked, or they are concerned how they will be perceived by others. Believe me, I can totally relate to this concept. At the time of writing this, I'm twenty-five weeks pregnant with my separated husband's baby, with our curly haired toddler at my feet.

Not exactly judgment free material, but whatever....

Confidence is a choice.

In fact, it's thousands of choices over and over again, and a big part of that, is choosing to not allow your self-worth to be dependent on anyone else's perceptions of you.

MANTRA

My self-worth is not dependent on someone else's perceptions of me.

Perceptions aren't real. Nope, they aren't and they are all subject to personal opinion. If you move through life trying to control other people's opinions and how they choose to interpret things, you will miss so many of the good parts and spend your days trying to hustle for your worthiness.

Everyone is different.

Newsflash I know.

We have all walked different paths, met different people, formed different opinions and reacted to situations in our own unique way. Expecting everyone to enjoy the same cup of tea is madness, and if you have ever tried to take a tea or coffee order from a group of thirsty individuals, you will know that every man and his dog likes his beverage a different way.

The quickest way to feel unsatisfied and fearful within your life is to try and become something to everyone.

Moving through life hoping that everyone is going to like you is setting yourself up for a life of lack and disappointment.

One of the ways I used to beat myself up and limit my potential was to harbor many limiting beliefs about my appearance. I used to believe that getting rid of the fat stores above my knees would solve so many of my problems, but that's not how it works.

Can you relate?

Really, this knee issue I was harboring was merely a distraction from the real work. I was running from my shadows by focusing on my *flaws*.

It was far easier for me to believe that the reason that certain people may not like me, or get along with me, was because I wasn't physically perfect. Now I can look back, it was far easier for me to focus all of my attention on the shallow things that I deemed to be wrong with me, rather than stop for a second and look at the areas where I was hurting. Instead of being focused on learning to love myself just as I was, I used that energy to rip myself to shreds in the hopes that someone else would love me that way I needed to love myself.

Tall order that one.

I can't tell you the last time I looked at my knees with disgust, and my knees still look the same way they always have, although at present I can't see them over this giant baby belly. Who knows what's going on down there.

What's changed now is the yard stick I choose to measure myself by and it has **nothing** to do with the way I look and everything to do with how I'm showing up in the world.

Our differences and our beliefs are so valuable and so important, and nothing is more important than the belief you hold within yourself.

The best way to move through life is by always tuning

into what **you** want to do and if you make decisions based on **your** loves and likes you will never go wrong.

When *Becoming Brave* with your life and vying for the courageous, you need to move through with an energy that is true to you, true to your heart and always honor yourself. When you step out into the world and show up beaming from a heart-centered place, gifting the world what moves you, you are operating from within your power. Following what lights you up, celebrating what drives you and allowing happiness to be your compass. This together creates the map to contentment and a life lived in alignment.

It's time to start flipping the game on its head.

When your motives are clear you can be solid in your **why**. When that **why** is no longer dependent on other people's approval, like the cream on top of the milk, you are always going to rise.

There comes a time in your life where you must decide to put your desires out there and own them. There comes a time where you must decide that that little flame deserves to burn brightly and you are done dulling her down. There comes a time when you must decide that a life lived without daring is so much scarier than a life lived out loud. Even if you are the only one who hears the music, dance anyway because it's your song.

You don't have to share it all with the world.

You don't have to share a darn thing.

Not every brave maneuver is meant to be seen, in fact most of the big ones aren't visible to anyone else but you. As long as you know you pushed the envelope, that's all that matters.

I watched a TED Talk, *Teach girls bravery, not perfection* by Reshma Saujani and I could *not* agree more. Women have been raised to aim for perfection, whereas boys have been raised to be brave, take chances and embrace risk. Women, for years, have been encouraged to play it safe, color between the lines (boring), and this often results in us avoiding those pivotal moments, those growth opportunities unless we are guaranteed we won't look foolish.

How often have you not asked the question for fear of being the only one who didn't understand?

How often have you sat up the back because you didn't want to draw attention to yourself?

How often have you taken the safe option that you know you will succeed in over the road with potential risks that your heart is truly longing for?

I said, "yes," to all three of these questions and all three more than once, but those days are gone.

BRAVERY can take on so many forms and it's not always the big leaps that bring about the grandest results. I think the real power lies in crediting yourself for all of the moments where you *do* make the brave choice and you *do* make the call that helps you to grow.

It's putting your hand up and asking the question in a meeting.

It's having the conversation that matters even when your voice shakes.

It's taking the chance to live a little brighter, bolder and louder than what you did the day before and acknowledging yourself for being a badass.

It's the little steps where you risk imperfection,

embrace vulnerability and push up against your edge that really allows you to find your brave.

The Universe, God, your Angels, Higher Self, Elvis, Dolly Parton or whomever it is that you talk to, I know they laugh when we make plans and today, the Universe is having a right ol' chuckle at me because everything I thought I knew, was about to get thrown up in the air when the invincible woman that is my mum, was shown to be just like us and fragile.

My mum has always been the glue of our family, the one who quietly pulls us all together each and every day. The one who helps us all do what we do better and I know we are the people we are because of the amazing parents who helped shape my brother and me.

This last month, my mum has been faced with her very own set of scary circumstances and her health has come to question. With two mini-strokes in the space of a week, and a trip to emergency this morning, with a new heart condition, *Becoming Brave* was the only option I and we have.

You see, there's this misconception that bravery needs to come wrapped in huge monumental tasks, the ones that really blow your hair back. The big goals. The new businesses. The big dreams.

There is so much more to *Becoming Brave* that we haven't even touched on yet. What about the bravery you're forced to draw from when you are faced with losing someone you love. There's no real direction there, there's no one task, just the confirmation that bravery and courage can be silent. Sometimes, the bravest thing that you can do is to simply be there. Silently, stoically and do whatever you can to keep putting one foot in front of the other, or typing one heart felt truth bomb after the next. In these instances, priorities, vulnerability, self-care and compassion reign supreme in my book.

When the rug gets pulled out from underneath you and you are forced to re-evaluate everything you thought you knew. All the things that were once *sooooooo* important seem to look different in this new light. Priorities shift and adjustments are made. Surrender becomes essential. Some things are truly out of our hands and it takes immense courage to surrender and trust.

When I was advising one of my amazing clients to surrender to the moment recently, I think she thought I had finally lost my shit. In that moment, when all her senses were heightened and her gut was telling her to fight, the true strength and bravery would come in surrendering, accepting the moment and choosing another way.

It's OK to shift priorities.

It's OK to choose again, in fact, that's how we grow.

NEXT LEVEL IT

What is your why?

When you know your **why** you no longer need their approval.

Today, I want you to get clear on what that is for you, in whatever form feels right, and I would love for you to write it down and keep it somewhere you can see it daily.

Not on the back of the toilet door though, keep that for your times tables.

My
self-worth
is not
dependent
on someone else's
perceptions
of me.

12

SURRENDER AND THEN SURRENDER SOME MORE

Let's demystify **surrender** before we go any further. It's not the weak and cushy option many believe. It takes courage, character and one hell of a backbone to walk the road less travelled.

It's not about giving in, or giving up and saying, "TO HELL WITH IT ALL."

It's about choosing a more loving path, a path of less resistance; a path encumbered in faith and it may in fact, help you find your wings.

You know, I love a list so here are ten ways you can practice **surrender** in your life **today**. See if you don't feel a little more badass after adding a few to your day.

1. OWN YOUR PART IN IT

This is HUGE. When something goes wrong and it's your fault, own it.

- If you spill your coffee? Own it.
- If you slam your hand in the door? Own it.
- If you're late for a meeting? Own it.
- If you were wrong in the argument? Own it.
- Don't go looking for someone else to blame.
- You break it, you buy it.
- Stand up, hold and honor your place in the world.

I can totally relate to this one and that's why it's first. I can't even begin to tell you the sense of calm that comes over me when I own my own garbage.

Owning our story, even in the thick of it, especially while we are living it, is one of the bravest things that we can do.

2. FORGIVE QUICKER. SAY SORRY

Holding on to anger is like drinking poison and expecting the other person to die. Sometimes it's better to find peace than to fight for being RIGHT. The negative mind chatter and the backstory you are often giving the situation is exhausting.

**Say Sorry.
Let it Go.**

It is what it is.

Forgiveness is often easier said than done, especially if an old wound keeps opening up for you and you revisit the loss of trust frequently. If a blast from the past is messing with your happiness now, you have to ask yourself a couple of questions: *Has this person gone out of their way to show, and continue to show me that they are truly sorry and have committed to change? Am I really upset about the current situation, or am I judging this instance based on a past experience?*

Marianne Williamson said to me at an event in Sydney, when I asked her about broken trust, "At some point we have to release the issue and move on. We have leaving right's not nagging rights."

This was a massive lightbulb moment, because how much of the current events within our relationships are judged on face value and dissection of the actual event at hand, and how much of the hurt, or resentment stems from an old wound left untreated.

If I told you all the ways I love this quote we would be here all day, I will say this though, "It has magical powers on my soul."

The first to apologize is the bravest.
The first to forgive is the strongest.
The first to forget is the happiest.
        – Author unknown

---

3. TRUST THE PROCESS

There is a calm when you believe that everything happens for a reason. Having faith in something bigger than yourself is a beautiful part of life. Our faith gets challenged often, after all, having faith is about believing in something that you can't often see. So, how does one begin to trust the process? For every one of us it will be different. If you get thrown a curve ball. Welcome it. There is a plan unfolding whether you realize it or not.

This challenge is here for your transformation not for your destruction. A failure or hiccup is just a way of moving you in another direction. You choose how you see it. Sometimes things go pear shaped in order to keep the fire in our bellies.

When I first started to write this book, I was a few thousand words in when I lost the entire thing. Around 8,000 words, I believe. I considered throwing in the towel. I could have left it right there, but instead I chose to see this speed bump another way.

What if this was a chance to prove to inspiration and to the idea that I was serious about my message and that I was serious about making this happen? I was ready to work for it and if I hadn't lost the work, I may not have appreciated how much of my path and my experiences needed to come through me onto the pages. I had to trust the process.

4. Send Love to Those Who Need It Most

We all know those people who truly grind your gears. The more you allow them to wind you up, the more they control your energy.

If your boss makes you furious. Send him love and light.

If a family member is pushing you the wrong way. Say a little prayer for them in a way that feels right to you.

If you're no longer seeing eye to eye with a friend. Forgive them and thank them for allowing you to grow from this experience.

Trust me. You will feel much better.

Love conquers all.

Light envelopes darkness and sometimes the person who needs it most may actually be you. I know sometimes you give yourself a hard time. We all do, that's how I know, but coming down on yourself like a ton of bricks is no way to change the situation.

Imagine a scenario where you are feeling anxious. Instead of beating yourself up for not feeling the way you assume you should, imagine sending love and appreciation to the part of you that is feeling a little cautious instead.

For instance, my internal dialogue could be: *Naaaaaaaw Katie, I love the part of you that's feeling a little wound up over this upcoming event, it really shows you care, you're a bit cute. I love that you aren't sure about what step to take next, but things are going to be just fine, Princess. Just you wait.*

On the flip side, what about, for *f*ck's sake Katie, GET IT TOGETHER. You always do this*, doesn't quite lend itself to a positive outcome or a productive and feel good moment.

You are in charge of the internal dialogue so when you notice things are going down in your minds town, it's OK to change the script.

5. BE FLEXIBLE

Shit happens. It truly does. Life is not a cookie cutter pathway for anyone.

Be OK with a change in plans. There is no right and wrong way in this instance, just different options and ways to go about your day. Be open to change.

It might surprise you. That extra workload that Sheila from accounting lobbed on your desk could be key to a promotion and you could be thanking her before you know it.

6. What Can I Learn from This?

In every challenge, there is a TAKE AWAY. It's just whether you choose to see it or not.

Look for the lesson. Look for the way to grow and suddenly that shitty instance is a life lesson that will serve you for many years to come.

Ignore it and it will happen over and over again. That, I can promise you. The universe will keep giving you the same lesson over and over until you wise up and GET IT.

Have you ever noticed that you keep having the same issues with people? The same personalities, relationships and circumstances will keep coming your way until you find a way to stand your ground, know your worth and learn what you needed to learn. I have heard it spoken that every person that walks into our life is an assignment. This makes a lot of sense to me. We meet people for a reason, a season or a lifetime and no encounter passes without an imprint of some sort. Work relationships, friendships and intimate relationships all teach us something about the people around us, and more importantly, we learn about ourselves and what's important.

7. Can I Look at This in a Different Way?

It's all about perspective. In every situation, there is a choice. Instead of seeing a cancelled holiday as a disaster. Could it be the option for something else?

That illness that has been rocking your world. Could it be the very thing that saves you? That business that just didn't quite get off the ground. How many valuable lessons did you learn within that process? #Priceless.

Let's look at **criticism** and **feedback** for instance. If you took the comments as actual notes on who you are, your business or your project, you would essentially be doing yourself a disservice. What feedback tells you is about the other person, their opinions and their preferences. It doesn't actually tell you anything about you, so when you choose to look at the responses in a different way, you are learning so much more valuable information about your target audience and what their preferences are.

Pretty awesome, right?

- **Are you RESPONDING or REACTING?**
- **Do you find yourself snapping?**
- **Do you often say things without thinking?**
- **Do you feel attacked, misunderstood or ready to pounce more regularly than you'd like and this leads to rounds of verbal sparring?**

If you answered yes, to any of these, pull up a seat my friend, because there's a great chance you are reacting rather than responding. While they are both relatively run of the mill "R" words, the effect that the dalliance in both of these behaviors will have is very different.

When you **react** to something you are usually quick to jump. You are triggered by something that someone has said, or a situation. Your mind is usually elsewhere to begin with, and you become super quick to judge.

Instead of a well thought out, meaningful response you shoot from the hip with a mighty quick trigger finger. Your reaction is usually based on a story you have been telling yourself around the situation.

- *They never understand me.*
- *This always happens.*
- *They are determined to bring me down.*
- *I need to defend myself.*
- *They never listen.*
- *If I don't react this way they will never understand.*

With this sort of mindset, it's so simple to become reactive. You are already coming from a place of defense. A place of fear. A place of fight or flight.

There is another way to go and it's far sweeter for all involved. We are always presented with a choice and the path we take depends on our perspective at the time.

When you **respond** to something, you take the time to thoughtfully answer or choose your actions. You allow yourself time to copulate a considerate and compassionate response. It's not about taking minutes or hours, it may only take a few seconds, and those seconds can save relationships.

The key to being able to **respond** in a thoughtful and neutral way starts way before any encounter or event takes place. It begins with your mindset and deciding to come from a place of kindness and understanding rather than fear or negativity.

You have already decided that the way you wish to live your days is with a loving perspective and patience rather than reacting to what's unfolding around you. This will naturally flow over into every aspect of your life.

When responding, your thoughts around a situation may be something like: *How can I understand this better? How can I see this another way? I choose love instead of... They must really be hurting to react this way.*

There is a way through every block. A mindset of understanding rather than always defending allows life to flow with more ease and calm. If this feels like it is way off for you, or you are throwing a but, but, but ... you don't know what you have to deal with, then you are still in a reactive state.

The way people treat us is more of an example of the relationship they have with themselves, and when you realize this it's far easier to choose your words, choose your response and speak your truth. In doing so you will naturally feel more satisfied that you have represented your true self. #kindnessforthewin

We can't choose the hands we are dealt in this wild game of life, but we can choose to respond and play them in a way that serves us and never belittles others or our truest selves.

You know when you have stepped away from your core beliefs by the way it feels. You don't feel good when you hurt someone with your words, or you lash out reactively and that's because you are also hurting yourself. Every time you go against your authentic self it stings, and you don't need that kind of negativity and pain in your life.

Becoming **mindful** rather than **mind full** is something I work on every day in my relationships. Take my marriage for example. My husband and I had plenty of ups and downs, but I like to think that I was always committed to working towards fixing them. Regardless of the outcome, by me becoming aware of the stories that I was holding around situations like, he never listens, or he doesn't value what I do around here, changed the way we communicate, at least for a while. I will say this though, to live within a conscious relationship, both people have to be willing to come to the party. Awareness and acknowledgement is the first step to lasting change and it's important we each do what we can to break the cycle.

By carrying such negative beliefs around I was creating that behavior and those instances. By changing my thought process, I allowed every situation to speak for itself, and the snarky comments stopped. The communication opened up and wouldn't you know it, I was much, much happier.

This is a moment by moment thing, and commitment to change, not an overnight success story.

Full disclosure.

Some of our disagreements still ended in: "You are ...," "No, YOU are ...," and one that was a personal low point for me was, "*Eeeeeerrrr*, treś mature."

It's a process.

What holds us back the most in life is the stories we attach to moments that haven't even happened yet. If you choose to search for the best in people then that is what you will see. If you choose to believe that the world and those in it are out to get you then you will continually come from a reactive state with a fearful mindset, and be moving from a heavy negative place.

Give it a try.

Become a witness to your thoughts and see what stories you are carrying about the people in your world and see what mindset feels best.

Can I see this another way? Can provide so much insight.

Everything is open to interpretation, so if you are rubbing up against something and it doesn't feel good; ask yourself, *how can I choose to see this another way?* Here lay your answers.

The world needs a group hug, so let's kick it off right here. BRING IT IN LADY.

8. BE FLEXIBLE BUT PROACTIVE

If you don't get everything done that you intended, instead of letting it worry you and float around in your melon, allocate it a time somewhere in your diary. Get it out of your mind, onto the paper and clear that mind space for more important things.

There are only so many hours in the day and a fight against time is one rarely worth gloving up for. While we each may be our very own versions of a modern-day superwoman—we can do anything—but not everything at the same time. Understanding this can be of huge benefit to getting things done.

My diary is my savior and it truly helps with the allocation of my life's tasks and dream creations. If you aren't already using a diary, get on this STAT. Nothing gets left behind. Nothing is forgotten and you can relax knowing that everything is going to be taken care of and this in itself, is a brave move. Be flexible about the method, but head strong about the goal.

9. LISTEN TO YOUR BODY

Your body is a **messenger**. It is reporting back to you all day with things you need to know. ARE YOU LISTENING? If you are pushing, and stretching, and constantly filling up on caffeine to hide the tiredness, you're not listening.

If you're constantly looking for pills to numb the headache, eventually, you will come undone, you really aren't listening.

If you are choosing to ignore the hives that break out, the upset gut or the nervous twitch in your eye, then you are not listening. Your body communicates with you for a reason, sweet potato, it's a beautiful song and it's time to start listening.

I was a willing slave to the humble and oh-so loveable coffee bean for almost half my life, until January of 2016. I switched to decaf and holy hammer, wouldn't you know it, my overwhelm started to subside. My anxiety dropped like the ball in Times Square on New Year's Eve, and I don't think I will ever go back ... we shall see.

Disclaimer: I now enjoy a cup in moderation but it's a totally different vibe and most certainly not an everyday thing. *Shhhhh.*

For years, I ran from the fact that coffee was rubbish for my anxiety, but I was scared to give it up because I *needed* that energy fix. I needed and loved that little ritual, and while I was only having two cups a day, sometimes only one, the reality that it wasn't my friend wasn't something I was willing to face. Now, the change to decaf wasn't all rainbows and unicorns, some days there were headaches and tiredness. Other days, I was a little sleepy, I knew I was feeling that way for a reason. My body was telling me, woman, you need to rein it in and chill a while.

Convenient? Not always. True and smart advice? Always.

It's a brave move to stop running from the truth and your rig doesn't lie.

---

10. CALM YOUR FARM

Can I get an AMEN?

How often do you let outside circumstances affect your mood and outlook? If you are stuck behind a frustratingly slow driver and you begin to combust, throw F-bombs and threats everywhere and get all wild-eyed and road-ragey, the only person who is getting hurt by this is **you**. Those peeps are just cruising along, doing their thang and you are about to pop an eyeball while simultaneously losing the lining of your stomach. Take a breath and trust that you will get there on time. Your anger gets you nowhere. You will arrive when you are meant to.

I have a client Mel, who had the belief that she couldn't get anything done at work unless she was in absolute overdrive. She didn't feel she could be productive unless she was running on fear and adrenaline and it was effecting her health, happiness, and outlook on life in more ways than you would think.

Her stress levels were always up so her body was releasing cortisol and storing fat as a safety mechanism. Her energy levels and motivation were dwindling because her adrenals were so tapped from being under the pump all the time. Her nutritional choices weren't supporting her goals because of the angst and fear factor involved in her daily work life, and her ability to digest food efficiently had gone right out the window with her meditation practice and self-care at work.

Mel and I, worked on unpacking a belief that, *busy* equals *productive* and the conscious choices in attitude that would support her new way to be. Daily goals were set. A little more structure put in place and a regular checking-in to maintain on target and on track.

When in doubt Mel would ask herself: *What would my Higher Self do in this instance?* Wouldn't you know it, the advice would always bring her back to the present, focused, assured and on point. WIN.WIN.WIN.

Life truly doesn't have to be a shit fight; you *can* choose an easier way.

Bravery isn't always loud, and it doesn't always appear as you would assume.

It's the quiet confidence. It's the silent decision, or the gentle stirring and inching forward of a dream being brought to life fueled by empowered passion. A vision or the only choice you feel you have.

Courage can take on many forms and it can be called upon in the most random of moments.

**Bravery and courage are quiet.
It's the insecurities,
the doubts and the fears
that are loud.**

Your brave move could be up there with the big guys for all to see, pushing the envelope, daring to spread your wings, or it could be as slight as the opening of a book.

The bravest thing you can ever do is always as simple as the next right thing, and that's all we *ever* have to do. If your plate is particularly full and your mind is especially noisy at any one moment in time, sometimes the bravest and most powerful choice you can make is to finish eating your meal and put the plate away. It could be deciding to get out of bed and have a shower. The bravest thing that you could possibly do in that moment, may be that you don't do anything at all, and allow it to be.

The only thing that matters is that it matters to you. As long as you've made the decision and as long as you know it's happening. As long as the driving force behind an action lights you up and it's a step towards a lighter or more inspired you, then *WELL PLAYED—*Brave Makers for the Win.

This **is your life.**

Don't be the person who said,

- **OK, I will do it** *when I have...*
- **I will make the call** *when I have...*

- **I will feel more confident** *when I have...*
- **I will be able to handle this** *when I have...*

NO. Non. Neine. Nich. NO.

I call bullshit on this story.

No to these, "when I have ...," in every language I can think of because you don't have to wait another day. You are already everything you need to be in order to do the thing.

Your talent library is kind of like your pantry. I bet your home pantry is filled with a whole bunch of spices or sauces that you have collected over time.

Almost everyone I know has acquired a whole bunch of amazing seasonings after random trips and moments of inspiration at the supermarket, and often don't call upon everything that's available right at their fingertips.

Those herbs, spices, and little jars of magic are all there, just waiting to be used to add a little more flavor to your meal. However, unless you reach into that cupboard and draw on what you have available to you and finally make use of this amazing array of culinary epicness, you are going to be eating a bland meal of beige rice and broccoli for the rest of your days.

You can add some flavor.

You can draw on what's already there. You have everything you have ever needed to have the most flavorful and brilliant meals you could ever imagine.

You just have to be brave enough to go into the pantry and add a little flavor.

- You have to try something different.
- You have to dare to add flare.
- To change up the meal from beige to badass.
- You have to **use the spice rack**.

In case you haven't been picking up what I am putting down, your inner workings are the spice rack and your amazing abilities and character traits are the spices.

You already have everything you will ever need to do anything you ever wanted if you have the courage to look inside your beautiful makeup and flavor your life.

Be the spice rack, sweet potato, use paprika!

If you haven't heard of the elegantly soulful, all-encompassing and inspiring entrepreneur, Jessica Williams, please allow me to introduce her to you.

I've known Jess for many years, I've watched her not only transform herself and the way she holds her position in this world, but I have watched her try different things, lose faith in herself, get lost, rediscover her love and turn into an even more amazing human with her eye on the prize.

Jess's path hasn't been a direct route, but that's what makes it so flipping inspiring. Just like there are a thousand ways to make porridge, there are so many ways you can go about finding the right path for you. The path towards understanding yourself and your Spirit, and supporting yourself in your career isn't always as separate as you think. I believe that more often than not, the two go side by side.

After following the path that Jess believed she **should** be on (man that word grinds me when it's in this context), Jess decided to make a list:

- **I want to be creative.**
- **I want to have freedom in my role.**
- **I want to travel.**
- **I want to have responsibility.**
- **I want to be involved in health and fitness.**

Coming up stumps when thinking about how this could possibly come into fruition, wouldn't you know it the Universe delivered.

"At the time, I was completing a twelve-week fitness challenge with Ashy Bines. At one of the training sessions, Ashy's husband offered me a free challenge if I designed some graphics for them. And, this is where it gets crazy.

I soon became their first full-time employee. I began doing admin and a little bit of graphics. Then within six months it was amazing to see how the list I had written transformed into my real-life role.

By the end of the six months, I was doing all their creative work. I was also the Queensland manager. I was travelling around the state and hiring personal trainers to develop new locations. The role was obviously entirely focused on health and fitness. I had total freedom because I was working from home. Every single thing that I had written down had manifested and I thought, *Whoa, this is crazy.*

That was the first step to truly experiencing that I really could create a life that I love. That you don't have to settle for something less than you deserve. That was a big moment for me."

It doesn't end there.

I've known Jess for around six years, but I never knew that she experienced Social Anxiety because she hid it so well and me feeling all the feels that I was at the time, found that I now understood Jess on another level.

Even though on paper her role and life was ticking all the boxes (don't you just LOVE that?), she knew she was destined for more.

"At the time, I was constantly searching and trying to make something happen. I was doing a lot of courses, starting businesses on the side, travelling, moving interstate and so on. Yet each of these things never resulted in that big *aha* moment.

I found in the last year, that the more I invested into my own personal growth—worked through my own anxiety and connected with myself—the more things fell into place. That's when I began to relax, surrender and allow things to happen, the timing felt right and everything fell into place.

It's really amazing to be able to sit back and kind of go, OK, this feels right, work hard of course, watch it all unfold."

Jess now has her own successful blog, *Create Live Grow* and holds events bringing women together nationally, creates products with inspiring messages to make a gal's life easier and she has done all of this by surrendering the plan and instead simply following the crumbs.

The reason that I wanted to share Jess's story is because it doesn't have to all happen at once, and we don't always need to know the location of the ultimate destination, but we can create a totally wicked path if we hand it over, allow ourselves to trust our intuition and do the next thing that FEELS right.

NEXT LEVEL IT

Are you ready to go after what it is that **you** want in this life?

It is totally within you.

Why should you though, why should you get uncomfortable and stretch yourself a little further? I really want to help you answer this one, but that would defeat the purpose—insert awkward looking wink here.

- **Are you aware of what your** *WHY* **is?**
- **Do you know what moves you?**
- **Do you know what drives you?**
- **Do you know what gives you those butterflies?**

Have you ever sat down to think about what a few of these BIG emotions and goals mean to you? To set out to create waves of awesome within your life's beach, you need to define what's important within your life and hone in on the way you want your life to feel. Just like Jess created a list for the aspects that were important in her career, we are going to look at the feelings you want to embody within your life.

You might have different words, but through my research—three words tend to be on the list for most of us—health, happiness, success.

Have you stopped to think about what these words look like for you? Grab a pen and paper and get defining because you may already have all these things; you just haven't acknowledged it yet.

How about I jump on the couch for a nanosecond here.

For me "Health" is king. It means being able to move through life with ease, but to break it down even further, health means: Having enough energy to enjoy my days. Honoring sleep and going to bed before 9:30 p.m. most days. Having access to nourishing, fresh foods, and movement. I like intentional movement at least four times a week. Being able to move through the day pain free.

Allowing alone time and space. I really need space.

"Happiness" is an inside job and for me, means: Being able to spend time with my family and to hug my son and make him laugh.

Freedom to do the work that I love. Discovery, adventure, trees. I need nature. The ocean: it's the salt air, it's the symphony of the sound of the waves.

Meditation and alone time. My friends, an all-girl gang and giggles.

"Success" is contentment in whatever I choose, like: My freedom of choice. My son. Consistency with my work. It's the little things like getting a newsletter out, keeping on top of emails or creating content. Moving every day. Alone time. Money in the bank to always be able to pay our bills. Not a sexy truth bomb I know, but none the less.

So where am I going with this?

I know what I need in my life to have it feel good. To have it ring true and to allow me to feel **confident** with my decisions.

If I stop honoring all that makes me FEEL good, then I don't have the ability to show up strong. I don't have the ability to soften. I become rigid and strung out. And, the likelihood that I will be able to make brave and ballsy choices diminishes considerably.

Did you notice I need alone time? A LOT ... HA. I do. I unapologetically do. It's what keeps this Katie train chugging along. Silence for me is part of the action that is required to live my wildest and wonderful life. No doubt about it.

What are *you* going to do *now*, that ensures your life is filled with the things that light you up and supports you?

**Find your three words,
and break it down.**

P.S You can bump it up to five, or if this style of reflection and life assessment really resonates with you, Danielle Laporte, founder of *The Desire Map*, dives into something very similar to this with such beautiful detail and it's well worth the time.

Stop
shoulding
all over
yourself.

13

I'm Not Brave Like You, I'm Brave Like Me

When I think about the bravest women I know, they all gain admiration from me for very different reasons.

Bravery is in the eyes of the beholder, and what might feel like the biggest hunkin' leap of faith to one person, might seem like a walk in the park for another. It's all subjective and it's all relative. Never underestimate how the smallest change in one's direction could be the boldest move they've ever made.

Since deciding to push the boundaries and embrace the **fear**—it's not like I've been looking for ways to push the envelope and conquer my fears—but I've been super aware of when that all too familiar feeling arises and I've made a conscious effort to lean in.

It's been a beautiful learning curve leading to a ton of self-enquiry and often a few harsh words from myself. When I notice the feelings envelope me, I acknowledge it. I see if this is my ego talking or if my intuition is saying, *Lady, back the bus up—pronto—this is a NO-GO.*

There's been some pretty interesting outcomes, let me tell you. I recently booked a ticket to see Rob Bell in Sydney with my beautiful friend, the event fell on my birthday and I thought that would be an epic way to celebrate. Upon purchasing this longed-for ticket, my tummy flipped and the fear rolled in. My mind started to race and I thought, *what have I done?* I started freaking out about leaving my family on my birthday, having to drive to Sydney, worrying about the traffic, the cost and all the other little things that came along with a day trip planning.

Was this my intuition piping up letting me know it wasn't such a crash hot idea? Nope, it was my ego trying to talk me out of an amazing experience and I ain't buying what she's sellin'.

I'll be sure to let you know how it all goes, but needless to say, I am totally pu1mped, my ego can calm her tits and I'm even going to buy his new book while I'm there ... yeah, that'll show me.

Update: I never actually got to go because my beautiful boy decided he needed a trip in the ambulance with major respiratory issues. We left the hospital with an asthma plan, a happy boy, and a promise to make it up to my beautiful friend who is the most understanding person in the world.

I have been incredibly fortunate to be born in this world and live my life. I live in a safe neighborhood. I come from a great family. I have never had to deal with racism. Most of the harshest judgments I've had to face so far in this life have come from within.

I have been open about the fact that I often experience

all the fears. I became a Mindset and Motivation Mechanic, to support women to be anything they wish to be, and to empower them to see the gifts and choices within their own thoughts. I have spoken in front of hundreds of women on *Rocking Your Confidence*, and I even wrote this little book you might have heard of called *Becoming Brave*.

So, what happens when a woman who has based her career around helping others nail a rocking mindset, has to admit she needs help from a doctor and anti-anxiety medication in order to regain control of her own?

The shit hits the fan, that's what.

In January of 2016, after managing, or not managing my anxiety for almost two years, I finally sobbed to my GP, "I think it's time. This is beyond what I'm capable of handling. My tools are no longer working and I no longer feel like I can do this on my own."

After advising this for quite some time now, I must say she looked rather relieved.

To admit that this wasn't something I could handle on my own was freaken hard. I grappled with so many things.

How can I be a mindset coach, when I can't even talk myself out of a fearful fucking situation myself?

- *What is this going to mean for my business?*
- *What will people say?*
- *What if they change who I am?*
- *I feel like a Fraud.*
- *What if I never feel normal again?*

It was rough, and all I knew at the time was that all of THAT was better than feeling like this.

I knew the answers would come in time and I had to trust my gut that right now was the time to move forward. I want to share what I figured out as my answers to some of the hardest questions I've ever had to face in my career.

Showing up every day to fight a war that no one else can see is still the most badass things you can do.

How Can I Be a Mindset Coach, When I Can't Even Talk Myself out of a Fearful Situation?

When you have a chemical imbalance, from trying to be strong for too long, all the tools in the world aren't going to be able to help you feel at ease and calm within your life. Even a life raft can get ripped to shreds in a storm of 60-foot waves.

Part of being a great coach, is knowing when to refer on, and knowing when someone needs extra support or specialized guidance.

I knew what I was starting to experience wasn't right so I changed it, and *that* was the responsible choice.

Was it easy?

HELL NO!

What Is This Going to Mean for My Business?

I am my business. If I'm not in a good place, then neither is it. My anti-anxiety medication has bought me back to a place where I am excited about my business again. I can get through the day without overanalyzing every little detail. This is a huge win.

So, what did this decision mean for my business? It meant that I could keep doing what I loved.

What Will People Say?

Who cares. People will always judge and I have to do what's right for me and for my family. If someone has anything negative to say about me feeling good about myself, and the way I am living my life, there's the door. I wish them well.

What If the Tablets Change Who I Am?

You know what, being scared shitless over the smallest thing changed who I was.

Being unable to focus changed who I was.

Worrying about every little thing changed who I was and I didn't like it one bit.

That crazy part of my life was NOT allowing me to live my truth. My medication helps me to BE WHO I AM. Making this decision has helped me to be able to use the tools I have spent so many years putting together. Making the decision to do what I needed to do to take my power back was not a decision I took lightly. If you had seen the tears that I cried to my doctor, you'd have thought I was signing over my life. Little did I know, I was getting my life back.

I Feel Like a FRAUD

Ohhhhh, GOOD ONE.

Just because I am a coach, doesn't mean I can't get anxious. If you are a doctor, you aren't immune to getting sick. If you are a nutritionist, it doesn't mean that you won't have food issues. If you are a personal trainer, it doesn't mean that you won't ever lack the motivation to get your ass to the gym. Dentists still get tooth aches. Teachers still have to learn things. Psychologists get depressed. Some hairdressers still have terrible haircuts.

No one is immune to struggle. I still think that showing up every day to fight a war that no one else can see is still the most badass thing you can do. I know I'm a brave *mofo* because I know how freaken scared I was to make this decision. I know what it took for me to get to a place where I could.

WHAT IF I NEVER FEEL NORMAL AGAIN?

What is NORMAL? Normal is a dryer setting my friend, and I have no interest in being likened to a home appliance. Albeit an incredibly useful one and possibly if you could set me to wrinkle free I'd be even more receptive.

I am so aware that I rebel against the status quo. I don't want to do what everyone else is doing. I don't want to follow the path that they have. I want to forge my own way and end up somewhere different. If that means I have to walk alone for a time in order to get to a place where the view is infinitely sweeter—I'll do it.

I went against the trend and made my e-course *Evergreen*. Experts say that's not the way to do it, but I created it to be available to women, so why on earth would I make people wait?

I've taken Facebook off my phone because I run my social media, it doesn't run me. I have so far refused to go on Snapchat because I feel I have enough going on. I slowed down on completion of my biggest speaking tour instead of riding the wave like suggested. I've cancelled workshops. Said no to speaking gigs and hibernated when I probably could have been spruiking.

If you tell me the paint is wet, I want to touch it to see just how wet it actually is and I'm so happy to be that way. Turns out, my son is too.

SCREW NORMAL

I'll tell you one thing, I was losing my happy. It was getting harder to find the light and that is not me. That is not *my* normal and that is so far from the person, I know, I am and the person, I love to be that I would have done whatever it took to get myself back.

I was meditating, eating organic and moving regularly.

I was journaling, sleeping well and feeling my feelings.

I was witnessing my thoughts, practicing gratitude and giving myself time.

I was loving myself in the midst of the chaos and spending my time with those I love.

I still couldn't shake the FEAR.

I saw psychics, energy healers and coaches.

I saw naturopaths, kinesiologists, and spent time with my friends.

None of it was helping because of a chemical imbalance that must have been going on.

With that little extra support, I can now use my tools and see my healing team and love my friends and embrace my normal. Living a life shrouded in **fear** and **self-doubt** doesn't cut it, and I am so proud of myself for having the guts to know when enough was enough.

For some people, making the choice to take anxiety medication may not be such a big deal, but it triggered a lot in me. I had to work through it and it was worth every second.

Something recently, I also grappled with was diving into *Nude Yoga*. The incredibly beautiful and passionate, Rosie Rees has been touring Australia for the past couple of years with her *Nude Yoga* sessions.

How **confronting** and **liberating** all at once.

There I was, sitting in my office, minding my own business when I saw this event was coming to Newcastle, and a couple of my friends were going to do it. I was instantly challenged. Not one to shy away from a growth opportunity, I thought that perhaps this was something I had to try. I was scared. There were feelings of fear that were swirling and as I went to lean in and jump, I couldn't bring myself to actually sign up.

I was baffled?

I'm writing a book called *Becoming Brave*, I should be attempting to conquer all my fears, right? I should be taking every opportunity to fly my *Brave* flag, right?

WRONG.

Sure, it takes a whole lot of guts to attempt a beautiful move like that. I admire the women who do it and I think it would be a spectacular experience, but I don't feel like I need to do it.

I'M NOT BRAVE LIKE YOU, I'M BRAVE LIKE ME

I don't think that I need to do that in order to help my spiritual growth along. Maybe one day it will feel like the right fit to me, but it didn't that day and it still doesn't now, and that is totally OK.

We all are moved by different things, and we all need to honor the calls that excite our Spirit and for me, that day sitting there in my elastic pants, I wasn't called to act. It affirmed for me that my souls moved by different things and in turn, my soul will move mountains.

I don't believe in walking the path that others have simply because they have ended up somewhere great. What you'll uncover about yourself if you commit to creating your own map is far more valuable than the coordinates to someone else's castle.

One of the bravest and courageous women I have ever known and had the honor to share words with is Laura from *LINK & Luna*. Her sort of Brave is the stuff that legends are made of.

I first came across Laura through Social Media and was instantly captivated by her wit and fast talking (writing) sense of humor. I slowly sought out to "like" all her platforms, and love every one of her beautiful images of moses baskets and gorgeous planters. On Mother's Day, Laura posted a picture of her son, Linik (Link) and my admiration for this amazing woman grew exponentially and infinitely and I knew I had to connect with her.

"Link was due to be born on the 18th of December. Instead, he was born sleeping, on the full moon on November the 14th. I had longed for a baby my entire life. I have a pretty tumultuous past, I've experienced a lot of emotional trauma and abuse and I just felt like my life would finally be complete; I could finally breathe properly, and I would finally be loved and never alone, when I had a baby. My whole life had lead me to

Link and in a single moment, it was all taken away. Link is an incredibly powerful soul and we are so deeply connected. I truly believed that he was destined for incredible things. I thought he would change the world (am I full of myself for thinking that? ha). In the early days, after he died, I could physically feel his energy and presence next to me, or on my chest as I lay on the couch. He has lead me through my grief so gently. There have been days where I have hoped and prayed that I wouldn't wake up, because it was all too much to bare, but overwhelmingly, he has given me strength, he has inspired me and has put me on a path that I was always destined to be on. I am finally living a life in line with my soul's purpose and I have never felt so fulfilled, because of him. I cry and cry sometimes because of the guilt that I feel for being so positive and having such a positive experience with his death, and for having such a good life after his death. My husband, James is quick to remind me, that it's not because of Link's death that I now live a positive, fulfilling, honest and abundant life, it's because of his existence."

Those words are some of the most powerful I have ever read: "... it's not because of Link's death that I now live a positive, fulfilling, honest and abundant life, it's because of his existence."

The transformation that has taken place for Laura because of Link's being has been huge. Their pregnancy was shrouded in fear, restrictions and all the anxiousness that comes with that all formed in the name of a love so big, for a little babe she was yet to meet. I am no stranger to love causing me to let my "worry" show and Laura being the woman she is found a lesson so great within the loss, I asked her to share in her words.

"Before we got pregnant, James and I had planned, almost twelve months in advance for the pregnancy. I stopped taking my anti-depressants, my pill, cut out alcohol, pain killers, gluten, dairy, sugar. I had suffered from severe endometriosis and was about to have my second surgery, but with the hope of a baby, I decided against the surgery and elected to try a new lifestyle first, just to see what happened.

After about seven months, of being **really** strict and **really** impatient, I woke up one morning, and realized that I couldn't remember the last time I had any pain. The endometriosis was gone and it hasn't been back ever since. So, my body was ready for a baby. The danger in being strict and balls deep in health knowledge, though (James was also studying Nutritional Medicine at the time), was that I became very rigid. I had literally healed my body just by eating certain foods and cutting out others. So, simple. So, genius I was, or thought, I was. With this confidence and the empowerment that I felt from taking control of my health, I became righteous in my views and I became so expectant of myself. Translated, I was really fucking anxious.

During my pregnancy, I became obsessive. I had NO idea at the time, because I truly thought I was doing the best thing for my baby. I desperately wanted the best for him because after all my life, the moment (being pregnant) was finally here. I was so scared of my entire life's hopes and dreams just turning to shit like everything in my past. I loved him so desperately that

I wanted the best for him, desperately. I was neurotic. I was afraid that if I showered too long; if the water was too hot, I would breathe in too much chlorine. I wouldn't wash the dishes without gloves and I **punished** myself every time I had sugar. I changed all hair care products and I only wore make up on special occasions. I felt so highly strung and if I'm being completely honest, the pressure and the stress I felt being pregnant, to be the best, to do the best for Link, to be fit, to be perfect etc. etc. etc. was intense.

I didn't cope. At all.

Unfortunately, it took such a tragic event to give me perspective.

I feel like next time I won't be so hard on myself, I'll ask for help and to be honest, I think everyone around me will be more supportive. I think part of being pregnant is feeling guilty for having to nap, or going home early, or calling in sick for work. Us, as women, feel as though we need to remain the same strong, independent and capable beings, but we don't. We should feel comfortable being however we need to be in any given moment.

- **Feel tired—nap.**
- **Want ice cream—have it.**
- **Need to take the day off—do it.**

And don't feel guilty.

Because you are creating fucking life and that is fucking incredible and it is NOT to be taken lightly."

The thing that stood out to me about Laura, initially, was the way she was using her voice. Her words were real, her words were always relatable and she wasn't afraid to go there, plus Laura also isn't afraid of the F-bomb which instantly endears me to a person even more. The way that Laura has turned the single most devastating event in any person's life in to a legacy, that would make anybody proud, is a testament to her. I had to ask her how she managed to navigate her way through this and her answer is bravery personified.

"I feel like my grief journey would have been so different if I wasn't spiritual. I have an inner knowing that this was meant to be. That Link was meant to change the world, it just wasn't destined to be the way that I had imagined. I have found peace in facing my grief head on. In fact, I enjoy the days where I grieve him the most because I feel closest to him in those moments. Life eventually gets in the way and although there's not a **single** second that I don't think about him, you push your grief to the side because it's impractical to always feel those emotions. I have to do the groceries, you know?

So, when Mother's Day rolls around, I let everyone know that I'm turning my phone off, I'm not responding to calls and I don't want to see anyone. I just want to sit with my grief and cry from the depths of my soul for the loss that I feel for my baby. It has also helped me to honor him. I talk about him often. I am not afraid to say, "I lost my baby." I am not afraid to say the words "dead" or "death". I find joy in my pain because he lives on through me, at my happiest and saddest times.

Honoring him through my business *LINK & Luna* (because he was born on the full moon), has also been incredibly special and something that has really helped in my healing, because it allows me to share him, and his message with the world, and it allows me to (hopefully) inspire and help others.

I think true healing happens when you help other people. I felt called to help others, almost like it's my duty because I'm one of the lucky ones who's had a positive experience and some people do it really tough, so I guess, I felt called to be a voice for those people."

And how does Laura see her future?

"I hope that James and I go on to live a healthy and happy life with a brother and, or sister for Link. I hope that I continue to create awareness and break the stigma surrounding stillbirth, and I hope that I continue to live an honest life (meaning that I'm always growing and evolving and being true to my life's purpose). I hoped even before Link was conceived, that one day, I would find peace. And, I thought that when he was born (alive) I finally would have it. But even though he died, and I lost everything, I still do. So, I guess the future is already here."

If you, like me, want to know more about Laura, check the back of the book for all her deets.

Bravery and the way you warrior up within your life will look so different for each of us and that's what's so epic about it. We are each going to face our own mountains. We are each going to be given circumstances and choices and the way we choose to interpret them is what's going to give us the trajectory of our life.

You can choose to let your circumstances make you better or bitter.

You can choose to let your life be about your inner warrior or worrier.

You can choose to focus on what's right or what's

wrong and that choices or those choices are only able to be made by you and you alone.

I think we are each showing up bravely on a day to day basis, but what I think isn't important, but what you think and give credit too is.

Next Level It

Recognition time. You, my friend, deserve a little acknowledgement, hell you deserve a *huuuuge* amount of acknowledgement, but I don't want to overwhelm you. We'll get there, though.

Where in your life have you been your **own** kind of **brave**?

It may be something you do each and every day that takes immense courage, it may be a beautiful one-off event, or a series of them? All I know is **bravery** creates more badassery than anything else, and it doesn't have to mean anything to anyone else, it only needs to mean something to **you**.

I'm not

brave

like You,

I'm

brave

like Me.

14

CONFIDENCE IS A DOING WORD

Y ou are never going to become confident in heels whilst remaining in flats.

Confidence is not a stationary object.

It's a verb, a *doing* word.

It loves movement and play.

It loves chances and small gambles.

It's always evolving, needs to constantly be challenged and is all about the *moments*. Confidence doesn't happen by accident. It requires conscious action, commitment to the cause and confidence rarely travels alone.

To evoke that inner confidence, you also need to tango with authenticity and vulnerability. Not in any particular order, I might add.

True confidence comes from a deep understanding of who you are as a person. It comes from doing the soul work, asking the big questions from yourself and being willing to follow through and trust the answers.

Getting to the essence of what moves you, what lights you up and what it is that you want from your time on this crazy ride.

I am not a great fan of labels. I also tend to rebel against stereotypes and I don't feel the need to be typecast or pigeonholed. The idea of fulfilling a certain niche doesn't *really* appeal to me and I know that goes against most of the advice you will ever hear around running a successful business. I get that. I'm OK with it.

I am many, many things, and I'm some of them more than others, and at times, I'm all of them at once. HA. That's OK with me. I define me and at times I am most certainly indefinable.

Again, I'm OK with that too.

A person who goes on changing, is a person who goes on growing.

I do, however, know that I love to write. This age-old art form has been a constant in my life for a few years now, and I'm so glad I reconnected with my words. What was rekindled as a perk for work has grown into a full-blown love affair. One that I know will last the ages.

When someone else referred to me as a writer for the first time, I fobbed it off. I tried to talk my way out of it the same way I used to deflect a compliment. I wasn't ready to believe it myself. I used to believe that the title, of a "Writer" was for those select few who were chosen to be published. I used to believe that I had to meet some certain criteria to cut the mustard. I used to give the power of validating myself to someone else and that seems about as sensible as a lizard on roller-skates.

I *am* a writer.

I am a writer defined by my own terms, and I am *still* a writer whether I am *officially* published, or not. I am a writer because I love to write and I get to know parts of me that are only accessible through the written word. I will always be a writer, whether I write books, or blogs, or even if I simply write in my diary.

You can be a runner if you run 1km, 5km or 40km. You can be a surfer whether you surf every day, once a month or once a year. You can be a cook whether you burn everything you make, or you create effortless masterpieces in the blink of an eye.

If you LOVE something, and it brings you happiness, don't allow someone else's definition to hold you back from claiming what's rightfully yours. Your Joy.

Your Joy

You don't have to be anything more than who you already are, to be anything you want to be.

"No one puts baby in the corner," and no one can define *your* happiness except *you.*

You are already everything.

Whatever you choose to call yourself. I hope you choose to be **happy**. Knowing who you are, and what you want doesn't just happen. The Universe doesn't owe you diddlysquat, you need to meet her half way. You need to ask the questions. Be open to the answers and be willing to hear the messages. We don't always get what we ask for, but we sure as eggs get what we need.

I spent many years closed off to the answers. I was so petrified of what I would hear that I feared even asking any questions. I was scared of being seen for who I really was, and petrified of not being seen at all. I would try and morph into the loudest most daring one in the room so that no one would look close enough to see how much pain I was in. Scared and unsure was my normal. I was hung-over most weekends. I wasn't present. I lost my license for a time and I was depressed, confused, bitter and full of regret.

Many years ago I lost my license. This, without a doubt, was a massive turning point for me and I'm still not quite over the disappointment of it all. I don't think I ever will be. For years, I blamed the circumstances. For years, I was scared to face the fact that my decisions led me to be in the situation that I was in, and the reality and part of the healing for me is that I had to own it.

The reality is that this was my mistake.

Mine.

I had a high range, Driving Under the Influence (DUI), and then an equally stupid, Driving while Disqualified just minutes after the court hearing, needless to say, I lost my license for three years.

I held and still hold **such** shame, guilt and so many emotions around this topic, but if it weren't for those mistakes, those lessons, that giant wake up call, I doubt I would have changed the trajectory of my life, and become the woman I am today. Hell, hath no fury, like a woman lost and trying to find her own way in a room full of people doing the same.

Back then, there was *always* a part of me that knew *this* wasn't *it*. This life I was moving through wasn't me, and this only fed the frustration and the anguish that was so evident to anyone who actually cared about me.

I couldn't be told though.

After enough signals from the Universe I decided ENOUGH. I decided that this was not how I wanted my life to go and I took myself out of the equation.

I had to create a cocoon for myself. I didn't answer my phone on weekends and I spent my evenings watching *Gilmore Girls* and reading. Instead of rocking home at 5:00 a.m. I was getting up to watch the sunrise and go for a run.

My priorities shifted, the gym became my club of choice and the world started to make sense to me again. I fueled my body with nourishing healthy foods and I started to learn about nutrition. I became a personal trainer and I changed my path. I took every course I could find that would help me be the best I could be in my industry and completed my Diploma in Fitness.

Those first few shaky steps moved into a trot, then a skip, and before you knew it I was running. Life began to feel manageable, joyful, like my own again and this opened the door to the world where I am now.

I took myself away from the distractions and I took action. I travelled the world as a personal trainer and stewardess on-board private super yachts. I came back and started work for one of the most successful women's fitness companies in the world, and I married.

Now, don't think it was all peace, love and mung beans

from here on in. I still had *such* work to do, although now, I was ruthless in pursing my new normal.

We also wanted to start a family and after four surgeries, which is now six, for endometriosis, I knew it wouldn't be easy but I didn't think it would be that hard.

We tried for over two years and it turned into a circus. For years, we spend our time hoping *not* to get pregnant, assuming that it's the easiest and most natural thing in the world, when the reality for us was something oh-so different.

After a year of trying normally, the fertility circus began. I was not only pursuing the natural and homeopathic paths such as acupuncture and naturopathy, I was also having ovulation inducing hormone tablets monthly, ovulation induction injections and blood tests every day for months. Constant trips to the hospital were all part of it and being monitored around the clock to try and help us bring a life into the world. I had tunnel vision and all my hopes and dreams were focused on bringing a beautiful healthy baby to us.

Finally, we fell pregnant. HOORAH!

I couldn't quite believe it. I walked into the toilet expecting another negative pregnancy test—I'd already done two that month which were negative, yet there it was—two little pink lines. The first time I'd ever seen anything so miraculous. It, for a few months, seemed like it was all worth it, until, everything that we fought so hard for was threatened.

Brendan was away in Fiji paddling when we were due to go in for our twelve-week scan. We had kept the pregnancy relatively quiet, because that's what you're meant to do, right? So, my best friend Jess, accompanied me to the scan so I wasn't alone, plus she was super excited for me.

We were sitting in the waiting room, talking about how I was going to make the announcement after the scan on Facebook. Whether we thought it was a boy or girl, and all those fun and milestone-y things that come with a first pregnancy.

There she was, on the screen, this perfect little tiny baby, moving around, happy and active ... at least, she was perfect to me. I loved her more than ever.

After the scan, we were told to wait in the doctor's room, where promptly a different doctor walked in the room to us giggling, only to deliver the news.

"I'm so very sorry, your baby is sick. I don't think it's going to make it."

I honestly felt like the air had been sucked from my lungs.

"But I just saw it, what do you mean. I don't understand?"

"Your baby has a tumour, which could be a symptom of Down syndrome, Turners syndrome and a few other conditions. It's called a cystic hygroma and is rarely conducive to life. We can do more tests now to find out exactly what the baby's dealing with, but I want you to be prepared. The tumour is covering her entire abdomen."

We were taken back into that room which was once filled with all my hopes and dreams, as they proceeded to insert a giant needle into my cervix to gather cells that would be sent away for testing.

My world stopped.

I was supposed to be sharing the news today of our **joy**. Instead, I'm in a room heartbroken, regretting that I didn't celebrate her every single day while I had the chance.

We made a few calls. I cried. I cried so hard. I cried a real ugly cry for days and the emotional rollercoaster continued. I wasn't willing to give up on our baby. I loved her and she was mine.

We found out that she didn't have Down syndrome, or Turners syndrome, or any other genetic ailment. In fact, she was genetically perfect, but the tumour kept growing. We also found out that she was, indeed a little girl.

We were given hopeful news, then news that would rip the rug away from my already trembling stance over and over again. For two weeks, we had scans and specialists every two days, until we were finally given the news that her once rapid heart was now slowing.

We lost our little girl at fourteen weeks' gestation to a cystic hygroma. She tried so hard but her little heart couldn't take the size of the tumour. We lost her.

We also lost part of me that day.

We named her, Gracie.

This was rough. I continued to work through the week we lost Gracie. I almost refused to acknowledge this was happening and even took myself to work the night I came out of hospital. I was too scared to be alone with my thoughts. Refusing to sit still and watch the life drain out of me. For six months, I carried on and threw myself into my work. They say that we teach most what we need to learn. Through those personal and powerful conversations that women have when they become real with each another—things started to shift. Not just for me, but for those beautiful clients I was working with.

- **I watched.**
- **I listened.**

I realized that if I really wanted to be a tool in the process of helping change the lives of those I had the joy of working with, I needed to go deeper. I needed to work on the mindset of the women I wanted to support more than anything because it sure as hell was rarely just about the physical.

I became a food and wellness coach; it was the perfect partnership with my training.

Your Wild Life was born.

I woke up one morning in July of 2013, knowing that I had to start a blog. I called it *Your Wild Life*. I wanted a place that was nothing but positivity and good vibes. A place where I could share with other like-minded women, write and connect.

So I did.

- **I needed to talk.**
- **I needed to process.**
- **I needed to connect.**
- **I couldn't find what I needed, so I became it.**
- **I created it.**
- **I took action.**

The fertility circus continued until I couldn't take it anymore.

I cried to my husband, "If this is the way I have to bring a baby into the world, then I am not meant to be a mother. A baby couldn't possibly come into this world with me feeling how I am. I am done with all the injections. I am done with all the invasiveness. I am done with sex to a freaken schedule.

I am done.

If we are meant to be parents, it's not going to be like this. I need to go back to yoga and I need to start drinking my green smoothies again and that will be it. OK?"

"OK," he replied.

I rook action.

I said no.

I fell pregnant with Archer, a month later, and this hurricane is the reason I can do what I do today. He is my professor, my rebellion and my wild on legs. He is the heart outside of my body, and I will forever be grateful, even on the days I struggle. It's not always about saying YES in this life, sometimes it's about saying NO.

Some of the biggest steps forward in becoming the woman I am today, have felt like I was taking a step backwards. My time in my cocoon. My monastery phase. My hibernation; that didn't feel so progressive, I just didn't know what else to do, so I took everything off the table.

It really wasn't pretty then, and just like the caterpillar, I legit felt as though I turned to mush so that I could rebuild and emerge a butterfly.

I really don't believe we go through these immense

times of transformation for our destruction. They aren't there to bring us undone, to rip us to shreds and leave us a shadow of our former selves. I really believe that we go through them to rise. We go through them for our transformation, we go through them to rise victoriously and see the world anew.

I am grateful for my lessons for they taught me what is possible. I am grateful for my struggles for they have shown me such contrast and I am grateful for the fodder of it all because it has been such a huge part in me being able to write this book.

I am taking the piles of shit that were once my obstacles and planting a patch of wild daisies and this will be my legacy.

Wild freaken daisies—they really are such a fabulously carefree flower—I don't know why they are often overlooked.

Let's change that.

NEXT LEVEL IT

So now, YOU, are you giving yourself credit for the places and the times you have taken action? Are you aware how proactive you are being in even reading this book?

The fact, that you picked up a book called *Becoming Brave* shows that you are ready to grab life by the ping pongs and make shit happen. Am I right? That was already an act of bravery right there whether you are willing to see it as that or not.

I do. I see it and I see you.

So where are you going to take this energy?

Where are you going to allow this momentum to flow?

You only have to take one step.

One step is all it takes and you do that over and over again.

Take a marathon for instance. Do you think that runner gets to the finish line of that race in one graceful leap?

HELL, TO THE NO.

That race is filled with thousands and thousands of steps, each just as important as the other and without each of them playing their part in that mission, you will either fall flat on your face or worse, remain still.

- **Do not pass go.**
- **Do not collect $200.**
- **Do not live the life of your dreams.**
- **Do not feel the joy of leaning in and being BRAVE with your life.**

Confidence requires action. My question is ... ARE YOU READY?

Take a piece of paper and fold it down the middle.

On one side write everything you do on a day to day basis. On the other side write down everything that makes you happy and feeling confident within your life.

Adjust your life accordingly

You
own
your
joy.

15

Where Fear Becomes Freedom

The freedom that comes with embracing the un-controllable and accepting it regardless is some truly potent shit.

Such a large part of my **fear** factor and I dare say yours too, has come from trying to control the uncontrollable. I'm no fortune teller, nor am I a psychic, and while these days my intuition has become my greatest ally, acceptance sets me free.

The need to control every element of my life is slowly dissipating and the freedom that that delivers instead is liberating. The freedom that comes with embracing the uncontrollable and accepting it regardless is some truly potent shit.

They say that those with an anxious mind are quite brilliant—I'll take that.

Our minds have the ability to come up with every possible path and outcome to a situation in .4

seconds flat. This Ninja like skill is a specialty of mine and I am learning to see it as such to give it the air time and appreciation it deserves. The energy it takes to forever be on guard, and the creativity one must possess to conjure up such dramatic sequences, while inopportune for sure, deserve to be respected. There's such magic in the way we view our fear and it truly is the key to a new way of understanding an emotion that's had us running from the hills or believing we are broken for far too long.

What if we no longer saw anxiety and fear as a negative, instead as our desire for a stealth like ability to be prepared for the future?

This perspective works; it's nourishing, supportive, and shows an element of emotional entrepreneurship for sure. Does it set you free, though? *Hmmmm*, not quite, but it does give this, often shady emotion the glow of a well-placed faux tan. I think we can still take it one step further.

What if your **what ifs**, were instead met with **acceptance**?

Stay with me.

Instead of worrying about bombing out at a speech, which could look like, *What if I make a ton of mistakes*, now it becomes, *I will accept it if it does*.

Worrying about specific health outcomes which might look something like, *If I get sick, what on earth will I do?* Becomes, *I am confident in my ability, and I will accept it if this happens*.

If you are worrying about going "all in" on your dream and having it fail now turns into,

This is worth the risk, if it doesn't go according to plan and looks different than I pictured, I will accept it if it does.

How different does that feel?

Instead of fighting the cause every step of the way, the fear factor dissipates when there is a faith in yourself and a faith in your ability to cope through any situation that is thrown your way.

You are capable of such greatness. We diminish that greatness and turn towards fear when we underestimate our own ability to handle what could possibly happen and the resilience we would show if it did. Let's just not do that, OK?

Acceptance is not a cushy, *fru fru* emotion. Acceptance is the real deal, it's the whole shebang. It takes such strength to trust the process and hand over the reins to a higher power and you, my friend, are more than capable, you might even be ready.

What do you say?

Throughout this book, you will have heard me talk about the signals. The energy that the FEAR FACTOR puts out and deciding what that emotion will mean for you personally. I know through years of observation and personal experience, that fear more often than not, can lead to greatness. We need it, it stretches us and it's there to be embraced.

The path that each of us takes to find our brave is so uniquely different, and I would love to introduce you to my friend Ofa.

Ofa is part of my Soul Squad, and one of the sweetest

and unassuming women you will ever meet. She's gone on quite the transformation lately, and I'm so effing inspired by her and her journey through sensuality, sexuality and the profound impact they play on us as women.

I asked Ofa what the turning point was in her life that signaled this massive road of discovery.

"I've always been fascinated by sensuality and femininity. There is something so intrinsically appealing to me about the magnetism and energy of women. I've explored different aspects of sensuality and femininity over the years. About seven years ago, I was drawn into the world of pole dancing and burlesque, and found the community of women so open, loving and friendly. I was amazed by how sexy and sensual the performances were and the appreciation of, and for women's bodies by both women and men in the community, that I joined an amateur burlesque troupe and performed a few times to paying crowds. Getting my kit off in front of a room of strangers was liberating, empowering and fun all rolled in together. It certainly forced me to get comfortable in my skin and was an avenue for me to express my sensuality.

Around the same time, my partner and I were seriously thinking about starting a family. By this point, we'd already miscarried, so had gone to see lots of doctors, naturopaths, and healers to help find out how we could "fix" ourselves. When I wasn't falling pregnant, I started to do a lot of research on fertility, tracking my cycle and trying to find the optimum time to have sex. This research which then turned into a broader fascination about how women's bodies work and so

I started doing more research into chakra and energy work, menstrual magic and sexuality.

The ultimate catalyst for me though, to dive deeper into sexuality, was when I miscarried again after attempting IVF about two years ago. My experience of IVF was brutal, both on my body and my emotions. It was honestly one of the most emotionally traumatic experiences of my life. I felt so broken, so sad, so disconnected from my body. I also felt really disconnected from my partner after this experience too. But I knew deep down inside that there was a better way to feel—a better way of living. So, I looked deeper into some of the research I'd already been doing around women's sexuality and found a way for me to really connect with my womb through tantric and Taoist traditions such as a jade egg practice. This practice had such a profound impact on me. I started to feel more connected to my body in ways that I had never before. I honestly felt like I could really feel my vagina and womb for the first time! It also made me realize that even as women, we don't talk about pussies or wombs, or how these are both sources of pain and pleasure. My curiosity was captivated from this newfound sense of connection with my lady bits. I've been learning about it and doing practices even since.

See for me, that is some scary stuff because I can totally relate to the disconnection following fertility struggles. There's nothing like your body "letting you down" to make you detach and avoid your feminine power completely.

Jumping head first into studying love, sex and relationships has been pretty scary. But the fascination is real, so I've remained committed to this path of learning. My mind continues to be blown by what I'm learning about my own sexuality and how it affects my relationships.

I think the scariest part of sexuality study for me, so far, has been confronting my fear around deep-rooted unworthiness and un-deservingness. I was only able to overcome this by bringing awareness to this fear. I've realized that my inner child has self-sabotaged some of my achievements because she feels unworthy of love. I've been able to really recognize and see this part of me. I've been able to send her so much love and compassion, and she now resides in the throne of my heart. Once again, this shift has had such a profound impact on my capacity for self-love and on my confidence.

The next hurdle is putting myself out there to share my experiences because I truly believe more people need to know how sexuality is intrinsically linked to our emotional states and ultimately how we operate as women (and men!).

My womb is such a source of power and pleasure for me. It also has strong connections with my solar plexus and heart energies that when I tap into all three areas—I am a powerhouse!

I am responsible for my pleasure. Not my partner or a fantasy. Just me.

I have a regular self-pleasure practice. My body truly understands different flavors of pleasure. My body holds so much wisdom and when I completely surrender to its sensations, my capacity for pleasure is off the chart!"

There's something magical that happens when you see people talk about the things that they are passionate about and it's certainly no different here. Ofa, glows!

I wish that we had these sorts of conversations more.

If you do have friends who you can talk with about our divine female energy, why not start a conversation about it? If you're not in that position, or perhaps aren't quite there yet, then I asked Ofa to share her advice for women who are feeling a little less loving towards their lady-ness.

"Our womanly bodies are so profoundly beautiful and wise.

We can learn to fully see her, appreciate her and connect with her on a deeper level.

Trust your body.

Stay curious to the signals she gives you.

I invite you to explore your sexuality and femininity in a more embodied way.

Because what I've learnt is that life can be so much more pleasurable when you feel a deeper connection to our sexuality, which I believe is the true essence of who we are as women."

Here. Here, Ofa ... here, here! What grew out of fear and hurt, quickly turned into curiosity which then turned into discovery, empowerment and ultimately freedom.

How. Good. Is. That.

Fear Shows up as a Chance for Us to Be Brave.

If we never knew what scared the shit out of us, then we would never know the joy of moving through that, conquering that or outgrowing that. If we never thought, *this is a bit of a gamble.* How could we live and enjoy the rewards of such daring adventures?

We need the contrast.

If life was filled with perfect days, we would learn to dismiss the sunshine. We need the thunder to appreciate the peacefulness of the warm summer rays and without it, we will never know real growth, from the earth or from ourselves.

Fear Shows up as a Chance to Teach Us Acceptance.

The wisdom to let life unfold in the manor it's destined takes SUCH courage. Acceptance is the bravest act of all. Surrender will never be for the meek. It will never be a sign of weakness or frailty, surrender calls on a belief system that can't be named for a force that can't ever be seen.

Acceptance of the uncontrollable when all our instincts have taught us to white knuckle it, control and fight is the ultimate act of bravery and badassery, and don't let anyone tell you otherwise.

Fear Shows up to Keep Us Safe.

You are here reading this book, because you at some point, have felt fear and you allowed it to keep you safe. Well played lady.

Not *all* fear needs us to lean in and rise. Not all fear is there to be tangoed with and hugged. Some fear is there to be heard and congratulated for its timing and foresight and applauded for its ability to stop you in your tracks.

"Go fear!"

That time you didn't walk too close to the rooftop of that building and fall over the edge? Fear kept you safe.

The time you checked both sides of the road before you crossed and waited that extra few seconds?

Fear kept you safe.

The time you didn't walk down the dark alley on your own? **Fear** in it's purest form and it all stems from you beautiful intuitive goodness.

A life without fear is never the goal.

A life deciding what that fear means to you is.

FEAR SHOWS US WHAT WE TRULY LOVE.

We have all heard the saying, It's better to have loved and lost then to never have loved at all. I would always seem to read this when my heart was at its most vulnerable and this is when it triggered me the most, but now I get it. To enter into love with something and to step into that arena, is entering into a contract that you are going to share your heart and attach to something that one day you will inevitably lose.

All relationships end.

Either someone leaves or someone dies and while this sounds flipping awful, it shows the level of vulnerability that comes when we enter into love. The fear of losing something is part of any love lesson, but would you choose not to enter into that loving experience to avoid the fear and the hurt of having to say good bye? I would never give up a single, true and heart felt hello. The hello that made all other hello's so much sweeter, because one day it will be replaced with goodbye.

Would you?

Didn't think so.

Next Level It

Let's throw a little GRATITUDE party for our pal, FEAR.

Sit down with a pen and paper and jot down all the times where your Fear has been the best thing that could have surfaced.

Give yourself time and space to really think about it and one by one see where in your life you are really grateful for your Fear, and see where it was actually giving you a platform to find your BRAVE and have a super proud moment.

There's nothing like clarity and the power of a **reframe** to see something in a brand-new light.

A life
without fear
is never the goal.

A life
deciding
what that fear
will mean to
you
always is.

16

YOUR WAY OR THE HIGHWAY

Right, Soul Sister, here we go. I have defined Fear and Bravery six ways from Sunday, and by now you probably see fear in a different light for which we shall all say, HOORAH, and charge our heels to the floor in an awkward attempt at boot scooting.

This is all fabulous. I am totally down for the celebrating, but what does **fear** mean to you? How have you chosen to perceive this four-letter word, and how will you choose to allow it to be represented within your life?

My intention for writing this book, was to see if together, you and I, could make some magic. Through my words, and your vision we could start to put the wheels in motion to make this far off dream a reality. Fear is nothing more than information. It's an emotion based signal put in place by a thought process, or seven, and when you choose to see it that way, the whole plane shifts.

Women, and their capabilities amaze me on every

level. We feel so deeply, aim so high, love so openly. Don't even get me started on the magnificent temples that are our bodies.

The levels to which we can reach are limitless; however, I've got to be completely honest that things have changed when it comes to what I set out to achieve since Archer rocked my world.

I know this may not be true for every woman, but my goodness it's true for this one. I am still the same vibrant women with hopes and dreams and desires that I was "PB" pre-baby. I still have the same drive, the same work ethic, albeit I fit my business around my life now, not my life around my business, but the fire still burns—hot.

I still take pride in my appearance, but I am super proud to wear my good trackies on errands, and to coffee, these days because I feel content and confident in them. They are comfortable. They have a dropped crotch that makes me feel like a badass, like I'm one of the cool kids and I can do life easily in them. They work for me, I don't think they caught the eye of my husband at the time, but *whatev's.*

There are some things that have definitely changed, but while I've seen these changes portrayed by some as negatives or a downside, I see these changes as beautiful additions to my life.

One of the biggest and most influential changes that have come about are boundaries. These essential guidelines I've put in place since becoming a mother came about by listening to my soul's whisperings, and have helped me create the life I have, and am so very proud of.

My mental state is a top priority, right up there with Archer's happiness. The two go hand in hand, if you think about it. He needs mamma to be sane and smiling, and I need to know I'm doing the best I can by him to feel happy. WIN.WIN.

I *still* want to believe that I can do all the things.

I *still* want to believe that I can do everything and even more than I used to PB, but I have come to the liberating realization that I can't. I cannot, and will not attempt to do all the things at once. I now vibe to the tune that I can do anything, but not everything at the same time, and that is fine by me. I can still run a business and be a kick ass mamma bear, but I can't stay up late to do it. I can still train and feel fit and strong, but I can't attend **all** the wellness weekends, I once wouldn't have thought twice about saying "yes" to. I can take Archer on fun adventures and help him learn nature most days, but this also means nutritious yet uninventive dinner's and that's the pay off.

I have other beautiful factors at play in my life every day and within every moment invitations present themselves to me allowing me to choose who I want to be.

I'm not shackled to my life, adding a person hasn't taken away any of the part's I love about me, it's helped me reinvent myself in new and exciting ways. I can now get so much done in the two hours that Archer sleeps, it freaken astounds me sometimes. Emails, blogs, phone calls, bookings ... when my mind is on the prize, I've got tunnel vision, baby.

I choose my life and in that I need to love and own the choices I make and the moments that get my attention all day, *erry*-day. That's my job.

That's who I am, and thinking about my life this way makes me happy. We can do anything we want in this lifetime, so let's not add the pressure of having to do it all at once. Let's enjoy the moments we're in without always feeling the need to wear all the hats and then find a pair of killer pumps to wear with them too. Get yourself a pair of good trackies; get your swagger on, embrace the moment you're in and be proud of all you've achieved today. Know that, **that** is enough.

If your day is not bringing you joy, what can you do to add joy to your day? That's as simple, or as complicated as you want to make it, friend.

Getting to a place where I was more accepting of my life and its beautiful twists, turns and changes meant wearing fear as a back pack and committing to seeing the hike through.

At times, I didn't know if I was ever going to reach the peak, but by choosing to see fear as a sign that I am on the right track and that each new somebody-save-me-now situation was here for me to grow. It gave me the permission I needed to thrive despite my fear. Not only did I thrive despite it, I truly believe it was because of it and it showed me over and over, that I don't need anyone else to come save me, that in fact, I am the only one who can save myself, and you are indeed the only one who can change things for you.

If I hadn't wanted to turn the light on my fears and take the shadows away, I don't think I would have kept searching. I know I wouldn't have picked up a self-improvement book, and I'm damn sure I would never have begun to meditate.

So many of the best things in my life have stemmed from a bat shit scary place.

Everything that I have ever felt amazing being on the other side of, preceded chaos and angst. Every speech I've ever made had me trembling beforehand. Every time I've shared more of myself than I've felt ready for, I've been greeted with celebration and sisterhood. Every time I've wanted to bail but stayed the course instead, the result has been infinitely more powerful.

Your **fear** is a chance for you to be brave.

It's a window into a world where you **made** it happen. It's the doorway to infinite growth opportunities and lessons. It's the culprit behind the saying that "nothing worth having comes easy," and it's the catalyst for your transformation.

If your path was nothing but good times and great rock and roll, would you really and truly appreciate it?

We need the challenge and we need the stretch. We need the room to be all that we can be, and **fear** in the traditional sense of the word gives you that.

How are you going to see fear now?

Not so scary, right?

If you decide to interpret those signals as nothing more than a chance to be brave, then woman you go have yourself a party.

Thought twenty questions were over?

Oh, sweet pea, we are *sooooo* not done yet.

Fear is just the trigger, the symptom, the signal, right?

Let's move into the outcome.

The result, the encore of what is available to you at the mere flicker of an eyelid.

BRAVERY

What does living a life that's brave look like to you?

Where will those brave moments lay?

Within the answer, to this question, is another beautiful layer of your belief system and that's your truth and your soul's desires.

In defining just what bravery looks like to you, you unlock the door to the chamber of awesome.

Let's get specific with the moments that will make you proud. Are they heart-racing, jump off a mountain with the elastic around your ankles kind of stunts, or are they subtler like pressing send on a newsletter?

Are they the bold maneuvers of signing off on your first home, or are they more like you on the sweet tippy toes of your weary feet as you make your way out of your child's room with Ninja like precision, so not to wake them?

Is it the launch of a brand-new business or taking the initiative to make that call?

All of these actions would evoke a feeling of fear in anyone with a pulse, but you, badass goddess rock star hybrid, you can totally do them, have possibly already done them, or can totally relate to what I'm putting down, and that is effing legendary.

Bravery rocks, but you can't be brave without first feeling the fear because without it, it's just action. The fear is the gateway for bravery and in that there lye your power.

HO-LY. SHIT. BALLS.

Can you see how passionate I am about this?

Do you know what this means? You just realized that in order to be brave, you first must allow yourself to feel the fear.

You just changed the game.

You just changed the rules and now I want you to Next Level It and put it down on paper.

Next Level It

Grab a pen, some paper that oozes possibility and let it all flow from you.

fear, in all its glory means to me...

fear shows up for me within my life...

I choose to see this emotion as my...

Bravery in my life is comprised of moments like these...

BOO-YAH!

In order to
be brave,
first you must
put yourself
in the path
of your
fear.

17

SUCCESS TOWN

The personal investigation and discovery of what one particular word and what it truly meant to me changed all the things. It changed my approach, it changed my middle, it changed the outcomes and the flow on effect from my business to life, it has been life-changing to say the very least. Even with that epic pitch, I still think I'm underselling it here. Here's another hefty and oh-so true truth bomb.

We must define success on our terms, if we truly want to succeed.

Pfwoooor... lofty, punchy and poignant all in the one little love bomb of a sentence.

We all want to feel successful. We all want to feel satisfied and accomplished at the setting of the sun each day. Throughout our days, we are presented with many paths, many options and many ways to achieve our success. What success is meant to look like. How it's meant to roll out and what path we are meant to take if we want to get there.

I have been on this freight train to Success Town many a time, and upon reaching the destination not only didn't it hit the mark, but I felt overwhelmed, depleted, lost and often lonely.

There are a couple of reason's this was the case and that's because I was either following the model of someone else's success story, or I had in fact, outgrown my version of what it truly meant to be and feel successful. I was doing what I thought I should be doing, rather than what I wanted to be doing.

- **I wasn't living on my terms.**
- **I wasn't listening.**
- **I wasn't present and I would force the situation.**

If you have ever found yourself unsatisfied, unsure, lost or frustrated with or within your life then listen up because we are about to get all, Thomas Edison up in here and work on those light bulb moments.

When was the last time you took an honest look at the yardstick you are measuring up your life with?

When was the last time you examined your priorities, your motivators and your objectives?

When was the last time you acknowledged the things that bring you joy, celebrated the creative ways you live your life and got clear about what's important to you? If it hasn't been any time recently then there's a very good chance that you have outgrown your version of success, and it's time to re-define your life on your terms.

Insert totally jazzed girly squeal here!

WHAT DOES SUCCESS MEAN TO YOU?

Whether you are navigating the change from school to university, from university to the work force, from the work force through to motherhood, or back again just to name a few, the benchmarks you once measured *success* by would have changed. Life is full of transitions, of change and new beginnings so it's normal that your once comfy definitions of what you thought were important may now be a little too snug for your soul.

My long-awaited step (or, thud as it may be) into motherhood, from a bustling career as a successful fitness professional, overseeing and communicating with a team of more than eighty fitness rock stars every day, came as a huge shock to me.

I had finally been given the gift of a beautiful family, so why didn't I feel as fulfilled as everyone speaks of? Why didn't I get to the end of the day with the same sense of accomplishment I had so many days of my working life? Why didn't I feel complete, whole and like I'd finally arrived?

I felt as if I was failing at the one thing that I had wanted more than anything else in this world. How could this be? I loved my baby more than anything, but I was feeling like a failure every step of the way.

I yearned for the old me, the life that felt comfortable and the security I felt it knowing I was doing the right things. I wasn't used to being on my own all day, most days. I felt disconnected from the world, and myself, and somewhere in that beautiful rite of passage so many of us yearn for, I lost myself along the way. Or, so I thought.

It dawned on me after many long hard looks in the mirror, teary phone calls to my mom and even a trip or two to the doctor to let her know, "I think I'm losing my mind," I needed to redefine what **success** and achievements looked like on my terms. I needed to change the way I validated myself and give my life the importance it deserved. I loved my life, but I didn't like the way I felt within it.

When I got crystal clear about what I really wanted and what my real core beliefs were in this moment, I realized that those once irrefutable beliefs I had cemented at the foundation of myself worth, were no longer true for me. I had outgrown one version of myself and it was time to embrace a new one.

Completed checklists, successful meetings and smashed KPI's were no longer my focus and their inclusion a factor in a great day. Instead, a great day now entailed my babies' happiness, health, and the fact that I managed to keep him alive and happy the entire day. What gave me a feeling of success and accomplishment was when I could write for my website, when I connected with my community, and when I sent my newsletter out weekly. These things lifted me up, gave me a sense of pride and empowered me on another level.

What made me fulfilled was time with my son, and watching his milestones. Recognizing that all the trivial so called, small tasks throughout my day were adding up to the most important developmental leaps he would have, shifted my perspective from one of lack to one of importance and abundance.

I rediscovered that when I moved my body, nourished myself with healthy foods, made sleep a priority and made time to connect with friends, I was a better mother, wife, entrepreneur, friend and coach. I was a happier—a more whole version of me, and it was—as I defined it.

Everything changed when I changed the game, my life became mine again and with that came freedom and a huge flipping sigh of relief.

When we use external factors, those outside of ourselves to validate our success and fuel our worthiness we undermine our happiness and leave our joy and self-worth in the hands of someone else. We are taught this idea of "perform and reward" from our first days in kindergarten and even earlier in many cases. We still live this life of seeking validation in many areas across social media and that is why the platforms are so addictive. It's human nature to want to get LIKES on a post or article. It gives us the sense that we are accepted, understood and validated. It's addictive and ingrained and if we aren't aware it can become a really gnarly habit to kick and the quickest way to remain miserable.

Placing your happiness and your self-worth in the palms of someone else is the fastest way to ensure you feel stuck, or continue the path to a diagnosis of the Disease to Please.

Disclaimer: I totally just checked my Instagram and saw new likes on a post. This made me a little chuffed, I'm not going to lie. No one is immune.

Now, the things that I place emphasis on to instill a feeling of **success** within my life are achievable through me, acknowledged by me and created to support me, and I would have missed so much of the beauty of my now had I not taken the time to redefine what **success** means to me.

- **Through you.**
- **By you.**
- **For you.**

What if you weren't actually lost, you were just focusing on the wrong part of the journey?

What if you weren't unhappy with your life, you were just placing too much emphasis on old dreams, old goals and old ways of measuring your **success**?

What if the beliefs you had around what it meant to have a rocking life weren't even your very own? What if they were someone else's and you didn't have a chance to choose them for yourself?

What if you created a life that served you, lifted you up and was laced with the gems of inspiration that you truly want your life to be about?

That's available to you right now, right here and all it will cost you is a few moments of your time. The keys to your happiness may already be in your pocket, the answers maybe closer than you think.

You would think that if I would have realized the pattern, I could have so easily let it fall away and become a part of my past. *Pffffft* … apparently not, and this definitely won't be the last time.

Recently, I was on a plane back from Melbourne, the first leg of a three-state speaking tour and I should have been over the moon. I should have been content and satisfied, and celebrating, but I wasn't. I loved the event, it was a dream come true but in the lead up, I was saying YES to everything. I was doing all the interviews so as to not miss an opportunity, seeing extra clients so that I fulfilled my role to help. I was agreeing to host and collaborate on numerous workshops, all of which was going to take me away from my son and my family and I really, really missed him.

I was sitting in that airport waiting for my return flight home and my anxiety hit fever pitch. *If this is how success feels, then I don't want any part of it*, I remember thinking.

I boarded the plane, I opened a book I was reading, *The Accidental Creative* by Todd Henry, and it was a chapter on pruning your life.

Instantly, I knew what had to be done.

To live the life, I wanted to live I had to cut back on the things that were weighing me down and not necessary to my happiness. In doing this. I will make way for new and exciting growth and opportunities, and ultimately, I would flourish.

Immediately, I started drafting emails and messages in flight mode so that upon landing I would be able to instantly change my life and this feeling I had. I had been so caught up in the fear of missing an opportunity and believing that in order to be successful I had to grab every single thing that came my way. The mindset of "in order to be successful, you must be busy" set in. I really didn't want to disappoint anyone because so many of these opportunities did sound amazing.

As I waited for my luggage, I sent each one of those messages and emails, knowing that in my heart, what was meant for me would not pass me by. That it was time to get real with myself and so I asked the question, *what does success look like to me?*

- Being able to spend time with my son and family and create my roll around them.
- Having time each day to write.
- Making choices based on what FEELS right.
- Ticking off my TO-DO lists daily in my diary.
- Stretchy, day-dreamy possibility.
- Connecting with my tribe regularly, but only when I have something I'd love to share. Contentment.
- Saying no without guilt.
- Moving every day.
- Maintaining the space to create.

This is what success looks like to me. If I hadn't stopped to ask the question, I would have always fallen short.

Living a brave and wonderful life often requires these deep and pivotal conversations with our true-self. Without getting to the beautiful root of our core desires, we may wind up continually missing the mark and that's not a way I want to live my life.

That shit will keep you searching for that set of keys that was in your back pocket all along.

You need to define what **fear**, **bravery**, and **success** mean to you and live that truth on your terms. There is only one way and that's *your* way. Don't just go where other rad peeps have gone before you. Instead, grab a stick, whack some weeds and create a path to the top of the highest peak, on the gnarliest dream mountain and shout out something obscene letting everyone know that the view, from where you are is FUCKING AWESOME, and that you did it *your* way.

When we lose the need to seek approval from anyone other than ourselves we step into our freedom. We become the writer, director, the critic and the audience, the works. The question's then begin to look like: What will make me happy? Where is my curiosity taking me? What will bring me joy today?

Imagine, if you became a rebel with your own life?

What if you decided that you were going to live your life on your terms?

- **Embracing FEAR.**
- **Living BRAVE.**
- **Defining SUCCESS on your terms.**

You can have all of that. It's right here waiting for you. As a child of the Universe with dreams as big as the ocean, stop trying to fit all of your magic in a birdbath. You can't be stifled. You can't be contained. Let your rad-ness overflow and get beautifully messy with your life.

Fear, is nothing more than a chance for you to be brave, bravery is the door way to success and success is determined by you and your desire to live a life that makes you happy. That's as simple and as complicated as you wish to make it. ENJOY.

Next Level It

Here are some questions to help prompt you to define **success** on your own unique terms.

- What does **success** mean to me?
- Where in my life do I *feel* most **successful**?
- What activities and or actions give me the biggest sense of accomplishment?

- How do I want to *feel* at the end of the day?
- What actions can I take throughout my day to ensure that I evoke that feeling?
- How can I validate myself?

There you have it, a blueprint for what **success** really looks like for you, and how to achieve it.

Now, give yourself permission to live it.

If we
truly want
to succeed,
we must
define success on
our own
terms.

18

BABY, YOU SHOULD GO AND BACK YOURSELF

I could not; I COULD NOT finish this book without addressing the most significant step in becoming brave with and within one's life. Sure, I could have put it as "Step One" because it really is the most important, but you wouldn't have believed me at that stage.

Not a chance.

No Bueno.

If you're anything like me, before you were truly ready to wholeheartedly and unequivocally take the final step, you would need to understand all the other factors that are at play. Understanding the **why** often makes the **how** easier.

Peas in a pod.

When it comes to the big decisions, navigating the pivotal moments in our life, you know the ones we wish came with an instruction manual? There is one thing that you need to be able to do above all the other things that I have mentioned.

You Need to Back Your SELF

You need to **trust** yourself enough to know that the way you're feeling is enough of a reason to justify any outcome that you believe in. This whole belief system can grow to be rock solid; it's your foundation for everything else in your life. This important ability will carry you anywhere. It has very little to do with relationships but everything to do with having the courage within your life to do what makes sense to, and for you at any given moment. You and your decisions are under no obligation to be understood. EVER.

Write yourself the permission slip to be who you want to be, feel how you want to feel and live how you want to live.

You know the answers.

You know the next move.

You know what the right direction for you is. But, more often than not we let all the other "stuff" get in the way. You know the stuff I'm talking about, right?

- **The fear of disappointment.**
- **The fear of being wrong.**
- **The guilt.**
- **The reasoning.**
- **The comparison.**
- **The obligation.**
- **The what ifs.**

The **stuff** that we rationalize over our judgement and our intuition and in doing so, we diminish our totally witch-like ability to know what's right for us in every single situation.

Your feelings are your messengers, and sometimes they're not what others consider to be rational, but you don't want to be in the business of pleasing people. You're not living for everyone. You're living for YOU!

Can you now see, you amazing force of nature, that the second you try and rationalize your way out of a "gut feel" and a message from your intuition, you are telling your body and your soul that someone or something else knows what's better for you than you do yourself?

FUCK THAT!

Let's stop looking for things to make sense because in case you haven't noticed lady friend, things in life rarely make sense.

How will you know what is right for you though?

You will wholeheartedly know you have made the right choice in whatever situation you come across by the peace that you feel in your heart the second you've made it.

That is how you know.

Let peace and happiness be your guide.

Let contentment be the yardstick.

Instead of trying to always do what makes sense, look for the path and the decision that feels true for you in your soul, and that is all the freaken evidence you need.

Let's stop waiting for a light at the end of the tunnel to show itself and instead grab a freaken torch and light that sucker up ourselves!

We each have to choose our hard.

We each have to lay it all on the line in some way shape or form and stuff waiting for anyone else's permission to tell us that that sounds like a good option.

No one knows what's best for you other than the person who was born to make those decisions, and that's you.

You already have everything you will ever need. You already have the capacity to handle anything that comes at you, I mean look at your track record!

You already know exactly what I'm talking about in relation to your life; all you have to do is **back yourself** and trust yourself enough to take action.

- You will KNOW when the time is right.
- You will KNOW which way to go.
- You will KNOW when to say YES, but you and only you can be the one who takes that leap of faith.

That right there my friend is some seriously ballsy, bat shit scary stuff, but you're ready, and you know it.

It's not about waiting for things to get easier. Why not use the time and make it count?

- Are you with me?
- Are you in it?
- Are you ready to live it?
- You made it.

NEXT LEVEL IT

Now, it's is **all** about the **doing**.

Becoming Brave is about a decision.

- **It's a decision to throw caution to the wind.**
- **It's a decision to trust your feelings.**
- **It's a decision to put yourself first.**
- **It's a decision to be OK with whatever comes next.**
- **It's the knowing that you'll be OK with whatever outcome emerges and the courage to speak your truth even when your voice shakes.**

Becoming Brave requires your action, and now all that's left for you my beautiful friend, is to go do.

Get out there and live.

Live your life on your terms, with happiness as your compass, success on your radar, and fear along as a passenger.

You are the one in charge.

You are the one who calls the shots, and you and only you can decide that your happiness is worth whatever it takes, and you are made of whatever that is.

I have just handed you the keys to the rest of your life, now all you have to decide is where are you going to go to first.

My suggestion?

_____

Baby, you should go and back yourself.

_____

Thank you.

I want you to know I'm writing this not at the end of my journey when you'd assume most would consider themselves an expert. Instead, I am writing these words to you in my middle—through my becoming—embracing my during.

Don't discount the day to day stuff. Bravery lives in the seemingly mundane moments and the small steps that are headed in the right direction. There's something wonderful about the middle; the possibilities are endless, so much is left unwritten and it always gives you the power to create your own ending.

So it shall be. So it is. Let's rock on.

May we all *create* an *ending* worthy of *our during.*

ABOUT THE AUTHOR

Katie Dean is not your typical motivational coach, or a typical anything. She's a writer, motivational maven and the woman you want on your team. Katie is a new thought mindset mechanic, a researcher on how to debunk fear and is here to shine a light for women seeking confidence, clarity and courage. An Aussie girl from  the beach city of Newcastle, New South Wales she can be found sun kissed, smiling and never still for long.

What started as the blog *Your Wild Life* has grown into flourishing business that brings empirically based bravery approaches to women, entrepreneurs and change makers.

She does all this whilst being a Solo Mumma to two beautiful boys, the absolute loves of her life.

With a refreshingly no BS approach, Katie uses an interactive speaking bravura using plenty of humour, her worldly insights and tools to take her audience on an epic path of bravery and self-discovery. When you find yourself in the audience of one of Katie's events you know you are in for inspirationally filled Ah-ha moments that create real change.

Through her booked out coaching, national speaking tours, live events and loved-up writing, Katie is hell bent on lighting people up, laughing loudly and has created a successful business to help women unearth their brave.

Follow Katie:

@ktdean_yourwildlife
www.ktdean.com.au
www.facebook.com/ktdean.com.au

RESOURCES

Katie Dean

www.ktdean.com.au
Facebook - www.facebook.com/ktdean.com.au

Amy Mackenzie - Designing Her Life

Web - www.designingherlife.com
Facebook - www.facebook.com/designingherlife

Laura Grzelak - Link and Luna

Web - www.linkandluna.com
Facebook - www.facebook.com/linkandluna.au

Jessica Williams - Create Live Grow

Web - www.createlivegrow.com
Facebook - www.createlivegrow.com

Ofa Fitzgibbons

Web - www.about.me/ofafitzgibbons
Email - Ofa.fitzgibbons@gmail.com

CPSIA information can be obtained
at www.ICGtesting.com
Printed in the USA
FFOW02n0929260518
46821797-48991FF